DISCARD

Every Fifth Child:
The Population of China

Every Fifth Child:
The Population of China

LEO A. ORLEANS

STANFORD UNIVERSITY PRESS
STANFORD, CALIFORNIA 1972

To Dink, Nina and David

Stanford University Press
Stanford, California
© 1972 by Leo A. Orleans
Originating publisher: Eyre Methuen Ltd
London 1972
Printed in Great Britain
ISBN 0-8047-0819-3
LC 70-190527

Contents

Tables

Maps

Preface

Sometime in the distant past, the editors of this series inquired whether I would be interested in doing a population book – 'a kind of economic and social geography of China . . . rather than just another account of well-known statistics or a debate between demographers on the validity of the data'. The next year and a half went by with occasional correspondence, much of it expressing concern that the book be not too specialized, treating China's demography 'in the abstract and as a pure subject', and my reassurances to the editors that neither the quality and volume of data nor my style could make this a highly technical monograph. On the other hand I was not willing to do a 'popular' book on the subject. In an effort to resolve this contradiction, the title 'Every Fourth Child' was suggested for those who might be scared away by a more sterile heading, plus 'The Population of China' for those who are more fact and figure oriented. It is a reasonable mixture. That the title turned out to be 'Every Fifth Child' is incidental to this tale.

When concern over population has become universal, the implications of China's population are such that the interest extends far beyond the usual audience – it haunts the world leaders, frustrates the professional China-watchers, and intrigues many people who have only an understandable curiosity in the subject. Hopefully I have managed to write something that is scholarly enough, general enough, and interesting enough to make it palatable for both the professional and the lay reader.

Because the People's Republic of China has remained in a perpetual state of flux during the years of its existence to date, it is difficult to generalize its policies, conditions and attitudes. Inevitably the writer finds himself qualifying statements, excluding certain years, and (of course) overloading the manuscript with interminable 'probablys', 'possiblys', 'maybes' and other hedge-words. A paraphrase from Dante's *Inferno* is most appropriate for anyone contemplating the past, present and future of China: 'In the Eighth Circle of Hell, the forecasters, diviners, augurs and sorcerers endeavour to forecast the future which belongs to God alone. Condemned to Hell, their heads are twisted completely around, and they must walk unable to see where they are going.' And yet to write on present-day China and not to engage in the interpretation of the scarce and deficient data, or not to make judgments and estimates, would result in an almost worthless effort. I therefore do stick my neck out even though at times my head seems to be 'twisted completely around'. Furthermore, I suggest estimates that could have been easily avoided. I believe, however, that the only way we can make some progress in understanding what is happening in the world's most populous and enigmatic country is for those of us who spend so much time looking at it from the outside to make our evaluations and opinions available, and be prepared to accept the consequences.

In waging his relentless war on feudalism and imperialism, Mao Tse-tung likes to recite a favourite ancient fable about the Foolish Old Man Who Moved the Mountains: despite the constant jeering of the Wise Old Man who considered the task impossible, the Foolish Old Man and his sons kept digging at the two mountains that obstructed the view from their house. 'High as they are,' he would say, 'the mountains cannot grow any higher and with every bit we dig they will be that much lower.' I too had two mountains: to do this book in my 'spare time' and to do it without infringing on any customary extra-curricular activities. And like the Foolish Old Man, I laboured in bits and snatches . . . I hope the discontinuity of my work style is not reflected in the final product.

Although some of my colleagues may find the absence of scholarly source footnotes unbecoming, most readers I believe would just as soon not be distracted by them – the more so in this case since the majority would refer to undigested translations of Chinese Communist materials that would neither interest nor be readily available to the general reader. I have, however, included an appendix on the availability and nature of sources for research on China, and a fairly comprehensive bibliography of sources relating to the study of the country's population.

Administratively, the People's Republic of China is organized into twenty-nine first-order units comprising twenty-one provinces, five autonomous regions, and three municipalities (*shih*) which are placed at the provincial level. The municipalities control extensive territory outside the city proper and in this study the population of each municipality is included in the province in which it is located. Thus, in all the tables showing provincial breakdowns the populations of Peking and Tientsin are included in Hopei Province, and the population of Shanghai in Kiangsu Province. Furthermore, these tables do not distinguish between province and autonomous region, so that Sinkiang-Uighur Autonomous Region appears as 'Sinkiang', Inner Mongolian Autonomous Region appears as 'Inner Mongolia' and so forth. In general, place names are spelled according to accepted usage. Late in 1969 about one-third of Inner Mongolia was redistributed to five bordering provinces (Heilungkiang, Liaoning, Kirin, Kansu and Ningsia Hui Autonomous Region, reducing its population by about four million. Although this most recent administrative change is shown on the maps, it is not reflected in this study.

I would like to express my sincere thanks to William K. Carr, William R. Dodge, Tao-tai Hsia and Richard P. Suttmeier – four very busy friends who managed to take time to read the manuscript and provide me with some valuable comments. Dorothy Clark made editorial confrontations a pleasure rather than a pain and I thank her both for her editing and for her common sense. My special thanks go to Patricia A. Walsh who prodded me into agreeing to do this book and assisted me in many different ways in the course of my work.

In assuming full responsibility for any possible errors, misinterpretations, omissions and other follies, I would like to quote from the preface to *The True Law of Population* by Thomas Doubleday, published in London in 1853:

> As far as the author can ascertain, he has not, in entertaining the peculiar notions (in his book), run counter to any fact laid down and admitted by physiologists or nosologists; and, therefore, neither coming, nor desirous to come, in collision with any one, he may be readily pardoned for having, perhaps rashly, taken up views which, if they are unfounded, are at all events innocuous, inasmuch as, if not scientific in themselves, they do not seem to interfere with the science of others.

1 · The population record

It is paradoxical that China, a country with the most abundant historical population statistics, continues to represent the single most important puzzle to demographers. The establishment of the People's Republic of China in 1949 has not stopped speculation. On the contrary, the new role of China in the world community and the very immediate implications of the size and rate of growth of that country's population have proliferated the number of participants in the guessing game. They all agree on one point: China has the largest population of any country in the world. Surely the People's Republic will be under pressure to supply the United Nations with its own estimates for the size of her population and to provide some data on vital rates, age–sex structure, level of urbanization and other statistics on the characteristics of the population, making it unnecessary for the world organization to produce independent estimates for China. For the rest of the interested demographers, who have had to survive for almost fifteen years on most inadequate titbits of data, the debate on the validity and veracity of the reported figures will only intensify. This book should provide the reader with some appreciation of China's recent demographic history and a background necessary for the understanding of any figures that may be published, their broader implications, and the arguments that these data will undoubtedly elicit.

The census of 1953

When the Chinese Communists assumed power, they naturally had to rely on data inherited from the Nationalists. Using the records at their disposal they immediately proceeded to revise the country's population.

For the middle of 1950 the Liberation Army headquarters reported 492·5 million against the Ministry of Interior's 483·7 million; the State Statistical Administration reported a rather large jump to 556·6 million for the end of 1951; another revision by the Ministry of the Interior placed the population at 567·7 million as of the end of 1952. Still other estimates also fell within the general range indicated above, all of them essentially independent of each other, and undoubtedly guesses incorporating unknown assumptions.

The inaccuracies of the population figures were recognized by the new government in Peking, as was the need for something better, not only to provide population data for national planning purposes but also to register voters for the upcoming election. The obvious solution was a census.

Considering that in the advanced countries plans for a decennial census usually start almost immediately upon the completion of the previous count, the Chinese with six months did not allow themselves much time. They set 30 June 1953 as the date for the census. Most of the available details concerning this event come from an article by S. K. Krotevich, a Soviet advisor who helped the Chinese in its planning, organization and execution. Because all the current estimates of Chinese population are based on the 1953 effort, a close examination of this census is warranted.

Although initial responsibility was delegated to the State Statistical Bureau, actual implementation of the census was a joint effort of that Bureau and the Ministries of Internal Affairs and Public Security. Preparatory work started at the end of 1952. The problems faced by the authorities can be readily appreciated. Just how can an effort of such magnitude be organized and implemented in such a short time? It soon became apparent that much of the information ordinarily desirable from a census would result in unmanageable mountains of figures. Furthermore, a more comprehensive census would include additional questions which, in turn, would introduce problems of definition and interpretation. For example, some consideration was given to the inclusion of a question on literacy in the census schedule. The determination of who is literate in China, however, is so complex (literacy criteria differ for workers and for peasants) that the idea was abandoned. Another question that was considered and dropped to avoid possible embarrassment related to 'social background'. The Communists attach great significance to whether an individual's parents were peasants or workers (an advantageous background) or landlords or members of the urban bourgeoisie (a distinct handicap). It is extremely difficult (if not impossible) to outlive this background. Anticipating the many difficulties inherent in any census-taking effort in China, a very simplistic approach was adopted. Since the address of the household was already on the form, the individual had only to verify the information or to respond to four simple questions: name, date of birth, sex and nationality.

Several other basic decisions had to be made. It was clear that under existing conditions it would be impossible to enumerate China's tremendous population in a period of a day or two, and several months were allocated initially to complete the task. Since it was going to be a protracted effort, a means had to be devised to avoid double counting the segment of the population that was on the move, or temporarily absent from their permanent residence. The simple questions were thus encumbered by a complicated procedure. The head of household was asked to name all those living under his roof, whether present or not, while persons temporarily residing in a given locality were registered but not included in the final tabulations. All this was further complicated by the peculiarities of household arrangements, by the ambiguities of residence, by special problems posed by certain segments of the population such as boat people and nomads, and by an endless series of other large and small difficulties that had to be anticipated and resolved.

A very special problem for the census takers was connected with the determination of a person's age. The Chinese consider all infants to be one year old at birth and two years old with the coming of the Chinese new year. Under this system a child born on the last few days of the year will be two years old the moment the new year begins, whereas actually it is only several days old. In view of their efforts to simplify the census, it would have seemed reasonable for the Chinese to ignore this and other problems associated with compiling accurate age data, and accept an approximate age structure based on the Chinese system. Perhaps because any admitted inaccuracies in age could reflect on the census as a whole, they did not do this. In order to facilitate the determination of age of the population, all census workers were provided with a rather complicated table to transpose age from the lunar calendar (provided the individual knew his animal symbol, which reappears every twelve years) to the Western method of determining age. Table 1 is a translation of this.

During the short time available to them the responsible organizations managed to do a considerable amount of planning and preparation for the registration. Special registration offices were created in all provinces, cities, municipal districts, *hsien* and rural areas. Over two-and-a-half million cadres were trained to participate in some phase of the census-taking operation and activists were appointed from among the local population to assist in the task. Trial censuses were conducted and an intensive propaganda campaign was directed at the population to explain the goals and procedures of the census.

Although in most areas the work of registering the population of the People's Republic of China started on schedule, it was soon apparent that the prescribed timetable was not very realistic. In fact, there was an announcement at the end of 1953 that the census was only twenty-nine per cent completed. Progress continued to be so slow that by March of 1954 the census organizations were ordered to simplify the procedures and end the survey quickly. The census was finally completed that spring and on 1 November 1954 the State Statistical Bureau published the final tabulations.

According to this report, at midnight on 30 June 1953 the total population on the Chinese mainland was 582,603,417 [*sic!*], plus 11,743,320 overseas Chinese and 7,591,298 persons on Taiwan (Formosa), for a very precise grand total of 601,938,035. Of this total 51·82 per cent were men and 48·18 per cent were women. Also included in the initial report (and presented in subsequent chapters) was information of the provincial distribution of the total population, some scanty age data, urban–rural distribution of the total population, including the inhabitants in cities of over 500,000, and the distribution of the country's national minorities.

The crucial question, of course, is how valid are the reported results? Was China, in fact, able to take its 'first modern census' as claimed by the Communists? Was their claim in any sense realistic that, based on a nationwide sample check covering 52,950,000 persons, they were able to determine 0·255 per cent omissions and 0·139 per cent double-counting for a net undercount of 0·116 per cent when the 1960 census of the United States admits to an under-enumeration of 3·1 per cent?

If the problems and procedures associated with China's 1953 census were given to a Western-trained demographer experienced in processing population data only from statistically sophisticated countries, he would throw up his hands and discard the figures. There would be valid reasons for his reaction. No country, let alone one with almost 600 million people scattered over 3·7 million square miles of land area, could plan and execute a respectable census operation in such a short time. Strictly speaking, the Chinese did not even take a census, since most of the figures were obtained on the basis of registration rather than door-to-door canvassing. Some 8·4 million persons who lived in 'remote areas where communications were poor' were not even 'directly surveyed' but, rather, counted 'in other ways' – probably nothing more than estimates by the local authorities. Literally for thousands of years (with a few exceptions) the Chinese people have meticulously and often successfully resisted being counted; it would be surprising if some apprehensions did not persist. Although population information was of course the goal of the enumeration, the primary reason for the 1953 census, as throughout China's history, was nevertheless once again not demographic but political: the registration of people for the coming election and as a basis of control. The extension of the census-taking period to almost a year surely created innumerable problems almost impossible to account for – much less adjust for. And certainly the manual tabulation of millions of census forms by poorly motivated and sometimes barely literate 'counters' would cause our Western statisticians certain apoplexy.

Does this mean that the reported results of the census are so defective as to be unusable? No; most of the figures released on the basis of the census-registration are usable and used throughout the world. Because there is no reasonable alternative it is difficult to determine the effect of expediency in tilting the balance toward acceptance rather than rejection of the 1953 data. In all honesty, however, there are adequate factors which to some extent balance the criticisms discussed above and make acceptance not simply a matter of wishful thinking.

To subscribe to the Peking government's census, however, is not to be blinded by its claims. Needless to say, the reported omissions and duplications of a fraction of one per cent are absurd – hopefully reflecting only the ignorance of Communist propagandists – since a net error fifty times as great would still make the 1953 figures more accurate than any previously available. Of much greater significance is the question of intent. It is difficult to find a plausible reason for the census to have been anything other than a sincere effort to obtain accurate population data. By 1953 the Communists had secured complete control over the land, with both the Party and the government structure and power reaching down to the lowest administrative units and industrial and agricultural organizations. The lead time for the census was short, but the training effort was intensive. The two-and-a-half million persons who participated directly in registration of the population were supplemented by many more millions of 'activists', helpers and 'drum beaters' – enough people actually to disrupt production in some areas. The simplicity of the basic schedule and the length of time it took to register the population and tabulate the results would suggest that, at least this once, the Chinese tried to overcome inherent difficulties and arrive at a reasonable headcount of the population on the Chinese mainland. One can argue with their degree of success in coping with the problems, but not with their sincerity of intent nor with the dimensions of the undertaking. And that, too, is more than can be said for previous Chinese population statistics. Finally, no one can dispute the fact that the Chinese themselves use the same data that have been released to the world.

Earlier methods and findings

Despite general agreement that none of the available historical figures or series of figures can be taken at face value – most are replete with irregularities, even absurdities – old population statistics on China can be both interesting and revealing. In order to appreciate properly the significance of the 1953 census and understand the many problems Peking has been facing in trying to keep track of the country's population, it is well to backtrack and briefly review, at least in descriptive terms, China's historical population record.

Although some Chinese population data apparently date back to antiquity when the flood plain of the Yellow River gave birth to one of the world's original centres of civilization, it was not until the time of the Chou dynasty (circa 1100–250 BC) and the former Han period (206 BC–AD 23) that some systematic efforts were made to register and report the various segments of the population under the control of a particular ruler – efforts that persisted (with some interruptions) over the next 2,000 years. Questioning these unique statistics may seem ungracious; after all, isn't it enough merely that they survived? And yet, just because they are unique and 'because they are there', it is most tempting for any demographer or historian to play detective – to scrutinize, analyse, and interpret the figures.

Most analyses of China's historical population data start with the year AD 2 – a comfortable starting point for Westerners since it represents a meaningful bench mark from which to proceed. The Chinese reportedly numbered about sixty million at that time. From then until the beginning of the fifteenth century there were sporadic censuses and registrations from which blocks of figures or individual figures survived in various histories and dynastic archives. Scholars who have painstakingly analysed the available material do not always agree as to the details but express a generality that holds throughout China's history: population grew slowly during the more stable decades and declined drastically during periodic catastrophies. In any case, some fourteen centuries after the birth of Christ, when the Mongols were driven out of China and the Ming dynasty was founded, the population was again reported at around sixty million – this, despite the fact that in the interim there were periods when it was reported at over one hundred million.

Population registers, not unlike some of the more modern registration practices, were instituted by the first Ming emperor and resulted in an unusual record that provided annual figures for almost 120 years (1402–1520), until the system gradually deteriorated. While there is reason to believe there was population growth during this period, for most years the reported figures continued to fluctuate between fifty and sixty million.

In the middle of the seventeenth century, weakened by internal chaos, China was conquered by the Manchus who gradually consolidated their control over the whole country, to rule it for more than 250 years. Under the Ch'ing (Manchu) dynasty the Chinese initiated another series of annual population figures that lasted until they were disrupted by the upheavals of the Taiping Rebellion in 1851. Between 1651 and 1734 population statistics were tied directly to the very complex Ming fiscal structure and all estimates had to be derived from the reported number of registered *ting*, a somewhat confusing concept that is equated alternately with such units as family, taxpayers, adult males, etc. Naturally, population estimates based on the *ting* reports vary depending on the analyst's assumptions. The more reasonable estimates, however, seem to range from about seventy to eighty million early in the period and 130 to 140 million during the later years.

The historical figures that most intrigue demographers are those available for each year between 1741 and 1850 of the Manchu empire. They are derived from the *pao-chia* – an old system of control that was reinstituted during this period. It was an extremely complex system based on the successive groupings of households. Briefly, ten households made up a *p'ai*, ten *p'ai* made up a *chia*, and ten *chia* made up a *pao*. At the head of each group of families was an elected headman called a *p'ai-chang*, *chia-chang* or a *pao-chang*, respectively. All the information about a particular household – such as names, ages and occupations of all those living within the household, whether blood relatives or servants – was entered on a door tablet. Periodically the *p'ai-chang* compiled the information from the door tablets for the ten households under his jurisdiction and passed the compilation on to the *chia-chang* who then made up the detailed *pao-chia* register, which theoretically should have contained information for one hundred households. These then went to the *pao-chang*, to the *hsien* (county) magistrate, to the provincial governor and finally to the emperor.

In an official report to Her Britannic Majesty's Government of 1847, Montgomery Martin (treasurer for the Colonial, Consular and Diplomatic Services in China) described the *pao-chia* as follows:

> There is no country in the world where there are more opportunities of knowing the amount of population than China, as every district has its officer; every street, its constable; every ten houses, its tything-man; and every family is required to have a board always hanging up in the house, ready for the inspection of the regular officer, on which the name of every man, woman or child in the house must be inscribed. There is even a law to constrain Chinese householders to give a faithful return . . . When the master of a family, who holds land that is chargeable with contributions to the revenue, omits to make any entry in the public register, he is liable to be punished with one hundred blows . . .

Mr Martin was correct in that theoretically the *pao-chia* system should have provided an accurate data base; its main purpose, however, was not to provide population figures but rather, through collective responsibility, to ensure law and order, the payment of taxes and to exert other controls over the population. Thus the population figures which emerged from this organization of households were more a by-product of the system. The complexity of the system makes accurate interpretation of the data difficult and scepticism is reinforced by an imperial pronouncement in 1757 that 'the chiefs of the *chia* are generally common men who have never seriously assumed their responsibilities'.

USSR

Lake Balkhash

M

Urumchi

Kashgar

SINKIANG UIGHUR
AUTONOMOUS REGION

KA

KASHMIR

TSINGHAI   Hsi-ning

TIBETAN A.R.

Lhasa

NEPAL

INDIA   BHUTAN
                                    INDIA

BANGLADESH

K'un-m

YUN

BURMA

THAILAND

Population and
Administrative Divisions

International Boundary — · —   Administrative Boundary ———

Persons per square mile
0   2.5   25   130   520   1040

0   1   10   50   200   400
Persons per square kilometre

0   100   200   300   400   500   600   700   800 miles
0   200   400   600   800   1000   1200 kilometres

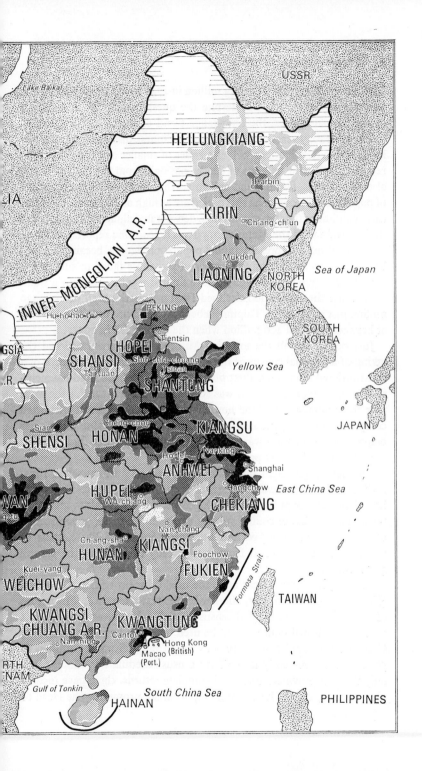

The reported increase from 143 million in 1741 to 432 million in 1851 is undoubtedly excessive, but despite the questionable dips and zigzags in the annual figures, the long-range trend of increase is reasonable.

The next sixty years were disastrous in Chinese history. The devastating Taiping Rebellion, as well as a series of smaller and more localized revolts, resulted in millions of deaths not only from the civil wars but also from floods, famines and epidemics that followed. Some estimates of population losses during this period are as high as fifty million. Under these conditions the statistical system deteriorated along with the gradual decline and fall of the Manchu empire. The *pao-chia* reports, which in theory continued to present annual population figures, became less and less reliable as an increasing number of provinces failed to submit the data. Once again specific figures have limited significance, but a trend is obvious: the population declined from a reported high of over 430 million just prior to the Taiping Rebellion to a figure usually estimated at between 375 and 400 million when the empire fell in 1911.

Just before its fall the tottering Manchu Government ordered the taking of a national census as the initial step for the establishment of a constitutional monarchy. First planned solely as a household enumeration in 1909–10, a headcount was scheduled for 1911–12. For the most part the enumeration of the households was made and statistics were compiled. However, the new republican government came into power before the headcount was completed and population figures were recorded for only a few provinces.

The new government immediately ordered its own census in 1912. Although this census was much more detailed, reporting the number of households and population for each province, it is difficult to imagine a bona fide population count evolving at a time when the government's control was still restricted and insecure. More than likely, most of the figures were obtained from data already available to the central government.

In 1928, less than a year after the establishment of the Nationalist (Kuomintang) government, another census was attempted. The nature of the results of the so-called census of 1928–9 is evident from the fact that the published figures could be used only as a basis for estimating China's total population – estimates which range from 445 million to 502 million. Apparently no uniform census schedule was adopted and only thirteen provinces furnished complete returns, three gave incomplete returns, and twelve made no report at all, prompting the Head of the Department of Statistics to observe that 'our country never had an accurate investigation of the population of each province'.

From the establishment of the Republic in 1911 until the Communist takeover in 1949 there were numerous other efforts to come up with a realistic population count of China. The Ministry of Internal Affairs, the Bureau of the Budget, the Post Office Department and the Maritime Customs Office, as well as other institutions, all tried their hand at producing national population figures, but partly because of only nominal administrative controls, neither the efforts to establish a unified registration system nor the attempted surveys and investigations gave any satisfactory population statistics. It is generally believed, however, that the population did grow at a modest rate during this period – perhaps at an average of one-half of one per cent per year.

Since there was no acceptable official population figure for the first half of the twentieth century, the various series that were produced were studied, revised and adjusted by both Chinese and Western demographers, geographers, historians, economists and others who were looking for a figure or a challenge. Lacking an acceptable authoritative figure, the analyst could select and adjust to obtain figures which accommodated his specific preconceptions and needs; the layman was happy with the popular, general-purpose figure of 450 million which was cited by the League of Nations and survived for several decades.

Until now discussion of the historical population series has only alluded to its inherent problems. Because there has been considerable continuity in the errors and biases, extending even into the Communist period, it is important to review the innumerable factors which in various ways have affected the nature of the figures. There are physical problems and human problems; biases of intent and lack of it; limitations caused by customs and traditions, prejudices and needs. Although not all these problems have been present to the same extent throughout the more than two thousand years for which statistics are available, because most of them have been perennial or recurring, time orientation is usually omitted.

The most obvious and basic obstacle to population enumeration is China's size. Since the time of Christ it has never been smaller than one million square miles, and the Manchu empire covered well over four-and-a-half million square miles. Admittedly few of the old figures even pretended to cover the entire territory under the tacit control of the emperors, but considering the nature of transportation and

Table 2 : China Proper : emended series of population statistics, AD 2–1953

dynasty and year (A D)	population (millions)	dynasty and year (A D)	population (millions)
Western Han :		Sung-Chin :	
2	71	1193–5	123
Eastern Han :		Ming :	
88	43	1381	60
105	53	1393	61
125	56	Ch'ing :	
140	56	1751	207
156	62	1781	270
Sui :		1791	294
606	54	1811	347
T'ang :		1821	344
705	37	1831	383
726	41	1841	400
732	45	1851	417
742	51	People's Republic :	
755	52	1953	518
Sung :			
1014	60		
1029	61		
1048	64		
1065	77		
1075	94		
1086	108		
1094	115		
1103	123		

Source: J. D. Durand, 'The Population Statistics of China, AD 2–1953', *Population Studies*, Vol. XII, No. 3 (March 1960), p. 249.

Note: Figures represent adjustment of recorded figures for China Proper, which embraces the eighteen provinces which lie between the Pacific Coast, the Tibetan Highlands, and the series of ranges forming the edge of Inner Mongolia. Professor Durand is well aware of the deficiencies of the figures and admits that the increases and decreases for some periods may be considerably distorted, but he feels that it would be a mistake to ignore these data and what they tentatively imply with regard to the population history of China. The emended figures in the above table do not necessarily correspond with some of the figures mentioned in the text. The 1953 figure differs from the census figure because of the exclusion of those provinces which lie outside China Proper.

communication, the terrain, the overwhelmingly rural scattered population and the heterogeneity of the backward and illiterate population, the existence of any figures at all represents an achievement.

Related to size is the inability to determine with any degree of assurance what areas were included or excluded in the population figures of a specific year in history. Not only the areas controlled but the effectiveness of the control varied from one dynasty to another and even from one year to the next. It was common practice to adjust available figures if for some reason current provincial reports failed to arrive. Given this situation, a comparison between any two years is rather risky.

*

One of the very important factors in assessing the reliability of any population figures is not only 'how' but also 'why' they were collected. Probably the most serious problem relating to ancient (and not so ancient) population data for China is that they were never intended to provide information for the sake of objective knowledge. Although many of the emperors considered population statistics to be extremely important ('bowing before the population registers'), of primary concern were the number of able-bodied males who could serve in the army or be forced into corvée duty on various construction projects and the number of persons able to pay taxes. Secondarily, the data also provided information for effective social control – so evident in the case of the *pao-chia* and (since 1911) the police registers.

As a matter of fact, in many of the historical series it is not at all clear whether the figures represent total population, or tax-paying population, or male population, or male population within certain age groups, or people 'who have teeth', and so forth. Since population registers were so directly related to taxation and military or corvée duty, many young males were willing to risk severe penalties to avoid registration. This fear of being registered has been so ingrained in the Chinese masses that efforts to conduct bona fide population surveys for demographic analysis met with great resistance during the 1930s and 1940s. Only in those instances of government aid to victims of some calamity or during periods of land distribution when there was a definite advantage to being counted was there the likelihood of factual reporting. At those times, an extended family with one or two married sons under one roof might record itself as two or three families.

The question of who was or was not included goes even further. The exclusion of women because they were 'not important' and of children because it was 'unlucky' to register them was fairly universal in many enumerations. But during certain periods and in some of the localities an interesting agglomeration of social categories would be missing from registers or excluded in special counts. The non-Han population (or ethnic minorities, see chapter 5) were considered to be barbarians and, therefore, seldom included. Also intermittently excluded were Buddhist monks and nuns, nobles, slaves, boat people, musicians, beggars and idlers, decorated military officers and so forth. Considering the margin of error in the reported data the omission of these groups is of little statistical significance, but it clearly reveals the relationship of population registers to virtually every consideration except demography.

An important point of contention for those who have tried to interpret Chinese historical population data stems from the fact that traditionally the statistics refer not to individuals or 'mouths', but to households or 'doors'. Accordingly, to convert households to 'people' it is necessary to come up with a reasonable conversion factor, or the number of persons per household or family. The size and character of a household is a moot point reflecting local definitions and customs that have fluctuated over the centuries. Does a household equate with a house – which may contain several families? Is a family that includes married sons, grandparents and servants one household? A simple example will demonstrate the possible error involved in translating from 'doors' to 'mouths'. If there are fifty million households, whether one assumes five or six persons per household will vary the total population estimate by fifty million persons and vary the final estimate by some twenty per cent. Since it is possible to hypothesize even larger differences in the sizes of households, inferring population size from household data is indeed a risky business.

Figures and figments since 1953

As already indicated, whatever their ultimate purpose might have been, population registers are a historical fact in China, and it was not long after the Communists assumed control over the country that they attempted to reinstitute the registration of population. It was these registers that were to provide the regime with the detailed regional and national statistics in the post-censal period.

Before 1953 there was no uniform registration system in Communist China. The endeavours on the part of the Ministry of Public Security to maintain a register of the population were limited primarily to the urban areas in which an effort was made to control migration into and between cities. Sporadic efforts to register births, deaths and population were also initiated in scattered rural areas. In both urban and rural areas, however, the coverage was incomplete and only occasional figures for small areas were reported, presumably on the basis of these registers.

In 1954 some provinces held conferences and drew up plans for a population registration system, but implementation continued to be extremely spotty. It was not until 1955, almost two years after the official date of the 1953 census registration and five months after the results were released, that a newspaper editorial proclaimed the need for a regular system of population registers. The editorial pointed out that results of the census were already outdated and that continuous registration should be instituted as soon as possible. It also noted an overlap in functions among the various civil administration and public security departments with regard to population registration: 'Only when the civil administration and public security departments coordinate their work and take uniform steps can the system of registration of persons be instituted in an orderly manner in cities and rural areas.'

In a directive of January 1956, the State Council tried to resolve the problem of divided authority between the Ministries of Internal Affairs and Public Security by transferring all the responsibilities for household registration and statistical work to the Ministry of Public Security. Although at the lowest administrative levels the system remained virtually unchanged, the civil affairs sections and departments of *hsien*, autonomous *chou*, cities, provinces and autonomous regions transferred not only all the registers and other materials pertaining to the population registration to the appropriate offices of the public security organs, but also all full-time personnel who were engaged in registration and statistical work. It is this system, then, that presumably supplied the Communists with the necessary population data during the years immediately following the 1953 census. The figures being cited by the Chinese officials and published in their periodicals during this period ranged from slightly over 600 million to almost 650 million, usually causing more puzzlement than enlightenment. For example, among the figures reported for the single year of 1956 were 603,230,000, 616,500,000 and 640,000,000. This variation would seem to indicate not only that there were no prescribed population figures which had to be used, but that, at best, the information was not accessible even to high-ranking Chinese officials, or at worst, there simply was no information for them to use.

Nevertheless, in June 1957 the State Statistical Bureau managed to issue what stands today as the only official series of national population figures ever to be published by Peking:

end of year	number (000s)	per cent increase
1949	541,670	—
1950	551,960	1·90
1951	563,000	2·00
1952	574,820	2·10
1953	587,960	2·29
1954	601,720	2·34
1955	614,650	2·14
1956	627,800	2·14

As in the case of the total population derived from the 1953 census, this series is also accepted and used by anyone requiring such data. And yet, considering the admitted difficulties in establishing the registration system, how could China come up with such precise figures, retrospectively reported in the middle of 1957? Their own explanation supports any doubts one might have: 'The figures for 1949, 1950 and 1951 were based on the trend of natural increase of our population in the past.' Both the Chinese admission that they have no knowledge of the previous growth rates and the nice round progression from 1·9 to 2·0 to 2·1 per cent per year point to some rather arbitrary estimates. The 1952 figure was derived from incomplete reports and adjusted to the end of the year. The 1953 figure was naturally inferred from the census. The 1954 and 1955 figures were 'based on the reports of provinces and municipalities', and the 1956 figure was based on similar but incomplete reports supplemented by independent estimates. Certainly nothing in these procedures instils great confidence in the figures.

To understand why a regime which strives to control the minutest details of an individual's way of life has been unable to come up with an accurate headcount, it is necessary to re-emphasize the importance of intent in relation to any effective system of population registers. It is very significant that the primary purpose in establishing the registration system apparently was not to maintain population records but to control the population. The first article of the regulations governing registration states: 'These regulations are enacted to maintain social order, to protect the rights and interest of the citizens and to serve socialist construction.' That is why the responsibility for population registers and records was not placed in the hands of the State Statistical Bureau or even with the Ministry of Internal Affairs but rather was assigned to the Ministry of Public Security and its various branches and offices which reached down to every administrative level.

It could be argued that although the Ministry of Public Security may not have been the most appropriate agency for maintaining population registers, at least it had the authority necessary to ensure compliance on the part of the people. Most Chinese, however, have a well-founded apprehension, even fear, about any contact with authority, generally characterized by the local cadre or the district police station. Usually of local origin and with little education, the policeman traditionally has wielded his power with a vengeance only a Chinese peasant could fully appreciate. It is easy to imagine, for example, that many individuals would take their chances on breaking the regulations, the importance of which would be difficult for them to comprehend, rather than to step voluntarily inside a police station to face an abusive official in order to report a death that may have occurred a month earlier. In other words, the prevailing attitude would likely be: leave well enough alone.

The almost incidental nature of the registration as a source of population statistics may be readily perceived by looking at the whole problem of rural statistics. Peking had to cope with three major difficulties before it could effect any substantial improvement in the calibre of its official statistics: (1) a shortage of trained personnel; (2) administrative deficiencies; and (3) traditional habits of thought which tended to militate against a conscientious regard for accuracy on the part of individuals directly or indirectly responsible for the collection and processing of statistical data. Local authorities were burdened with innumerable statistical forms dealing with crops, livestock, land utilization, manpower and so forth. The multiplicity of reports required, coupled with the pressure to get them in on time, created almost insurmountable problems for China's generally inept statistical personnel, so that despite the existing rules and regulations they were willing to take any imaginable shortcut and have frequently integrated population registration with other types of surveys, referred to as 'central tasks'. It is small wonder then that during the 1950s statistical journals were prone to complain that 'statistical figures are so lacking in accuracy that some figures are challengeable at will' and plead that 'falsification and blind estimates must be resolutely curbed'.

Peking, of course, was well aware of these problems and in January 1958 the Standing Committee of the National People's Congress adopted a new set of regulations governing household registration. In explaining these regulations the Minister of Public Security pointed out that they were necessary to 'perfect the system of household registration, since the existing system is still far from perfect'. He listed three main defects in household registers: (1) lack of uniformity in the system, not only with regard to the differences between the urban and rural registration procedures but between individual cities; (2) 'certain systems to be instituted either have not been instituted at all or have been instituted improperly'; and (3) changed conditions, making it necessary to revise or do away with systems that are obsolete.

The new regulations included special provisions covering persons in the armed services, convicts, temporary absence, marriage and so forth, and were relatively simple to satisfy. Information was usually entered on the basis of traditional households; registration books were to contain basic information on the number of permanent residents, as well as current information on births and deaths. Before moving, a person was to obtain a 'removal certificate' in order to be taken off the local register, and reregister immediately (within three days in urban areas and ten days in rural localities) upon arrival at his new place of residence. Specified time periods were also established for the reporting of births and deaths.

It is impossible to say if this new effort at population registers might have turned out to be an improvement over the previous years. The new regulations were soon overtaken by the ill-fated Great Leap Forward which raised havoc with the economy and in its wake left lifeless the infant statistical system that the Chinese had managed to establish. During the 'three bitter years' that followed, natural calamities, food shortages, the withdrawal of Russian aid and the disruptive effects of the Great Leap created conditions under which population statistics could hardly have concerned either the local statistical worker or the official in Peking. In the middle 1960s efforts to re-establish the statistical organization were slow and painful, and understandably concentrated on economic data more vital to China's recovery than population statistics. As a matter of fact, there were rumours of another census in China in 1964 – rumours that were mostly propagated by refugees who came to Hong Kong. Although some of them claimed actually to have taken part in such an endeavour, nothing was ever published by Peking and it would seem to be a most unlikely happening, since it is hardly possible to conduct a serious enumeration without widespread newspaper and radio coverage prior to such an event. Since the mass media never mentioned a census in 1964, it may have been simply an effort to update the neglected registers.

In any case, at the time of writing, China has not published any demographically-based figure of the country's total population. The all-purpose figure inevitably used in publications and speeches until 1966 was 650 million; later, 700 million became the most frequently cited figure and even more recently there have been some references to 750 million. These references to population did not appear in demographic articles (which are practically nonexistent), but in articles and speeches where the size of China's population needed emphasis – much the same way that references to 600 million people were used in the mid-1950s even though more precise figures were available.

The only other population figure that must be considered was derived on the basis of summations of individual provincial totals reported piecemeal during 1967 and 1968. They were reported without any explanation by the revolutionary committees during the height of the disruptions caused by the Cultural Revolution. Clearly the provincial authorities were in no position to obtain anything resembling accurate registration figures during those years. Thus the drastically rounded (to the nearest million) provincial figures (see chapter 4, Population distribution and migration) must have been approximations of unspecified date and unknown origin – perhaps an attempt to update the latest available numbers in the population registers. Nevertheless, the summation of the provincial populations produces a total population of about 711 million – not an unreasonable figure for the middle 1960s.

In view of the discussion in this chapter, the conclusion that China does not know the size of her total population should not surprise the reader. The only authoritatively begotten figure during the past twenty years came out of the 1953 census – and even its legitimacy has been

c

questioned. The registration system had barely enough time to produce a reasonable estimate before its destruction by the Great Leap and it has never truly recovered.

The contention that the Chinese government itself is without population data was recently verified in an unusually frank interview with Vice Premier Li Hsien-nien by a correspondent from *Al-Jumhuriyah*, a Cairo newspaper. In this interview, which took place in November 1971, Li was quoted as follows:

> We have been racing against time to cope with the enormous increase in population. Some people estimate the population of China at 800 million and some at 750 million. Unfortunately, there are no accurate statistics in this connection. Nevertheless, the officials at the supply and grain department are saying confidently, 'The number is 800 million people.' Officials outside the grain department say the population is '750 million only' while the Ministry of Commerce affirms that 'the number is 830 million'. However, the planning department insists that the number is 'less than 750 million'.

This absence of national figures, however, does not mean that the local levels too are completely without records. The leadership of a production team (a somewhat nebulous unit usually equated with a village) must know the size of the labour force, the number of children to be provided with some schooling, the number of families to receive a grain allocation and so forth. The margin for error, of course, widens as the statistics pass through the administrative levels between the production team and the State Statistical Bureau in Peking. The figures from about three million (some estimates are as high as five million) production teams must move up to about 500,000 production brigades, 26,000 communes and over 2,000 *hsien* spread out over twenty-six provinces and autonomous regions and incorporating a total rural population – depending on a particular time period – of some 600 million.

Under even the best conditions, taking toll of such masses would be a frightening exercise.

and the Confucian admonition 'To die without an offspring is one of the three gravest unfilial acts' was almost universally accepted, particularly since a male child represented the only available form of old-age insurance. With the extremely high infant and child mortality which prevailed during most years, a couple needed three sons to ensure the survival of one to adulthood; and to have three boys, that family would have to have had, on the average, six children.

On the other hand, there were a number of cultural, social and economic factors throughout China's history which had the effect of limiting fertility. Considering China's size and the diversity of her population, not all the factors were applicable across the board; but they were widespread enough to be significant. Among them were disease and malnutrition, which may act to limit fertility; the practice, by certain segments of the population, of coitus interruptus; female infanticide, which reduces the number of women to reach the reproductive ages; the common practice of breast-feeding babies for as long as one to two years, which reduces the probability of conception: inheritance patterns which limited marriage choices in order to retain family holdings; marriages delayed for financial reasons such as lack of dowry and gifts or lack of money for the purchase of brides for the sons; shortage of girls due to prostitution, concubinage and the already mentioned female infanticide; social approval of celibacy and disapproval of widows remarrying. All these inhibiting factors considered, the historical level of the Chinese birth rate for every 1,000 persons was more likely to be in the mid-forties rather than the mid-fifties.

Of particular significance was the practice of infanticide or child neglect – the postnatal mode of birth control. Although practised to eliminate defective and unhealthy offspring, it was primarily aimed at the female child who, as a consumer, could be a serious burden to the poor family, but because she would leave home on reaching marriageable age would be useless in perpetuating the family line and in the observance of filial piety. The practice of infanticide continued into the twentieth century, and as late as 1943 an official publication of the Nationalist government exhorted its readers to cease this practice, proclaiming 'the drowning of girl infants is to be prohibited'. Since fertility depends not simply on the numbers of people but the number of women in the population, the effect of infanticide on population growth could be significant. The survival of ten per cent fewer girls to the reproductive ages could reduce the birth rate also by about ten per cent. It is very possible the great preponderance of males reflected in Chinese distributions of population by sex was not necessarily the result of nonreporting of 'unimportant' females (and particularly female babies); there might, in fact, have been a real deficit of females.

The chances are that China's birth rate was more or less stable for many centuries with only minor regional variations. But specifically, what was the birth rate during the decades immediately preceding the Communist takeover of the mainland? Numerous estimates have been made; local investigations were conducted in many parts of China, particularly in the 1920s and 1930s. In some of the regional surveys birth rates were sampled directly; in other surveys data on age composition were obtained from which approximate birth rates were estimated. The differences in these surveys may just as likely reflect inaccuracies in the raw data and in the assessments as in the actual rates of fertility. Obviously no one knows for sure what the crude birth rate was, but probably most authorities would agree that a rate of 40 to 45 per 1,000 population is a reasonable figure and encompasses most of the suggested estimates.

Whereas the birth rate in China can be considered as high with probably only minor fluctuations over the centuries, the death rate is more difficult to estimate since it tended to fluctuate between high and very high, depending on the extent and intensity of frequent famines, natural disasters, military conflicts and widespread epidemics of such 'filth diseases' as typhus, cholera, plague, typhoid and dysentery. For the overwhelming majority of the Chinese population, death came without any interference from medical personnel, health facilities or drugs. Without straying into a dubious evaluation of the efficacy of Chinese medicine – a mixture of philosophy, science and superstition – it is fair to say that there were some legitimate traditional doctors who were true scholars and who contributed to the development, propagation and perpetuation of the art over several thousands of years. They were supplemented by a large number of practitioners of traditional medicine, some of whom undoubtedly had an appreciation of the human anatomy and physiology and were able to assist recovery, but too many of whom were aptly described as an 'incongruous, diversified, variable, motley group of physicians, leeches, empirics and impostors'. These were the quacks who gave traditional Chinese medicine a bad name and, in some areas, a reputation of being one of the nine lowest occupations in China.

During the first half of the twentieth century many dedicated people worked hard to improve the level of medical care in China. Through the efforts of missionaries and, to some extent, the new government in Nanking, medical schools were built, public health campaigns were initiated, local health departments were set up and even the Ministry of Health was finally established in 1928. All these efforts, however, were futile – at best affecting only a small proportion of the urban population. Poor communications, a faulty central administration and lack of personnel and funds prevented the general health of the Chinese masses from improving.

Since population registers and special surveys are much more likely to omit deaths than births, the collected data must always be adjusted – another very subjective exercise. According to Ta Chen, who conducted an intensive demographic survey of the Kunming Lake region in Yunnan and supplemented his findings with data from other estimates, the 1934 national death rate in China was 34 per 1,000 and the infant mortality was 275 per 1,000 births. These figures would seem to represent reasonable medians for China, with the death rate dipping into the high 20s during the better years and rising above the birth rate, for a net population deficit during particularly bad years.

Because of the fluctuating levels of mortality, an estimate of China's rate of natural increase for any one year would be almost meaningless, and yet one needs some perspective with which to approach the changes that have occurred during the past twenty years. Thus, as a point of reference, it is suggested that despite the wars, revolutions and frequent floods and drought, the population of China increased on the average of one-half of one per cent per year during the first half of the present century. It should be remembered, however, that because of favourable institutional and economic factors there have been many periods in China's history when her population must have increased at a much more rapid rate to have overcome recurring major disasters and to have reached almost 600 million by the middle of the twentieth century.

Fertility

Policies and programmes since 1949

When the Chinese Communists took over the reins of government and set up their new capital in Peking, the size and rate of growth of the country's population was undoubtedly not of vital concern to the new leaders. Furthermore, worry about overpopulation would have run contrary to Marxist ideology, which attributed human misery not to excessive population growth but to the maldistribution of income and other supposed defects in the existing social order. Since under the new society the productivity of the people was supposed to increase more rapidly than their number, the Communist leaders were reluctant to admit that the size of China's population could, in any sense, present a problem. They held that the wealth of the country was in the hands of the workers and peasants – and the larger number of hands could only create greater wealth. As late as April 1952, the *People's Daily* denounced birth control as 'a means of killing off the Chinese people without shedding blood' and as quite unnecessary since China was a country with vast unsettled lands and unexploited natural resources, and people were 'the most precious of all categories of capital'.

The results of the 1953 census were completed in the summer of 1954 and only a couple of months later, in September, the first note of anxiety was expressed by a prominent member of the National People's Congress – Shao Li-tzu. To appreciate the peculiarities of Chinese Communist etiquette, it is important to distinguish that it was not an official concern, but a concern by an official. Although his statement was most cautious, he was nevertheless criticized for advocating birth control. In his own defence he insisted that the dissemination of knowledge about contraception had nothing in common with either the old or the new Malthusian theory but was necessary to improve the health of mothers and infants, to advance the education of children, to allow mothers more time for work and study and in general to provide a happier life for all young men and women. This was to become the basic explanation of all future efforts to limit Chinese fertility, for in over twenty years there have been only a few statements admitting that a large population might have some adverse effects on the country's economic development, with Peking stoutly maintaining that 'moderating the birth rate is entirely different from restricting population growth'. Only when Mao mistakenly called for the expression of divergent views during the 'Hundred Flower' period in the spring of 1957 did a number of Chinese scholars express their concern over population growth because of its restraining influence on economic development.

Despite a certain sense of indecision, 1955 and 1956 saw a gradual acceleration in the number of articles that appeared in newspapers and magazines for and against birth control. By the summer of 1956 it became clear (although never official) that the birth control campaign had authority behind it and that the major responsibility for its implementation was assigned to the Ministry of Public Health. In August of that year, the Ministry issued a directive which stated that 'contraception is a democratic right of the people and the government should take every step to guide the masses and to meet their demands for birth control'. The final seal of approval was provided by Chou En-lai himself, who, in response to these demands by the people, included in a report to the People's Congress his own demand that health departments both disseminate propaganda and take effective measures for birth control.

The campaign, which reached its peak in the spring of 1957, was carried on with great vigour for a little more than a year. A Birth Control Research Committee was set up to 'coordinate experience and research in contraception', numerous educational campaigns were launched by local departments of public health, travelling exhibitions were organized and many hospitals and clinics introduced special facilities to give advice on birth control. Publications during that period implied that virtually everyone was involved, from women's federations, trade unions and the Red Cross Society, to cadres, school teachers and ordinary workers and peasants. Abortion and sterilization were reportedly available to couples who made joint application.

The campaign ebbed, just as it had accelerated, with overlapping articles both favouring and opposing family planning. Gradually the volume of arguments against any population controls overwhelmed the occasional reports of some family planning activities in a given county or plant. With the initiation of communes and the Great Leap Forward in mid 1958, it became obvious that China had reversed its only recently introduced policy of birth control. A large population was once more regarded as advantageous, and the vicious attacks on Malthusians, 'rightists' and 'bourgeois economists' who championed birth control again shifted into high gear.

The reasons for the 1958 policy reversal naturally led to much speculation in the West. Was it really possible that the Chinese themselves believed the proclaimed line that the country was now short of manpower? Certainly Communist propaganda had ostensibly succeeded in convincing the masses of even stranger ideas and the manpower-shortage philosophy meshed nicely, both with the labour-intensive projects that occupied every man, woman and child during the Great Leap and with the general optimism that permeated the country as a result of a successful harvest in the previous year. Nevertheless, it is difficult to conceive that the leadership which ordained the reversal was as convinced of the labour shortage as the mass media would have us believe, for the burdens of a rapidly growing population must have been apparent to anyone with any degree of judgment.

What might have happened had the euphoria of the Great Leap persisted is impossible to say. It was predictably of short duration; in 1959 China entered an economic crisis that focused all effort on survival – a dramatic change from the grandiose plans of the year before. For the most part there was silence on the subject of population growth but, as it turned out, the abandonment of the vocal programme of family limitation was not a complete reversal – it did not result in a campaign to encourage large families. On the contrary, contraceptives remained generally available, although mostly in the cities; birth control clinics continued to function; and although facilities were limited, abortion and sterilization continued to be legal and available (at least in theory) for those who requested them.

Beginning in early 1962, as the country was pulling out of the economic morass of the 1959–61 period, the Chinese resumed publication of articles encouraging family limitation to protect the health of the mother and the child. For example, whereas in 1961 the popular monthly *Women of China* did not carry a single item dealing with any subject related to birth control, in the last eight months of 1962 the same journal published six such articles. Although the new wave of articles which began appearing in the media were obviously initiated and implemented on orders from Peking, there was much less fanfare this time than in the campaign of the late 1950s.

The detrimental effects of early marriage were only a part of the earlier birth control campaign; now disapproval of early marriage ('a poisonous gas given off by the rotting corpse of capitalism') became the primary emphasis of the crusade. By passing the Marriage Law of 1950 the Communists had already raised the minimum age of marriage to eighteen for females and twenty for males, but at that time the reason for this law was not demographic; rather it was intended to replace the traditional, early, family-arranged marriage contracts with unions decided upon by the individuals themselves. The new proposals, by different authors, to raise the optimum age for marriage anywhere from five to ten years for both men and women were designed to limit the size of the family. None of these proposals was legally adopted, but arguments used in the campaign against 'the evil wind of early marriage' were most imaginative and made fascinating reading. They ranged from fairly straightforward explanations as to why early marriage is 'harmful to one's physique, health and career' to scare-tactics pointing out how dangerous it is to marry before 'various parts of the body have developed and matured'. Simply and to the point: 'Don't fall in love too early.'

As the general economy showed definite signs of recovery in the mid-1960s, the flow of articles on birth control once more slackened and it would have been easy but erroneous to have concluded that optimism had again eradicated all fears of rapid population growth. Although propaganda on birth control and delayed marriage in the mass media essentially disappeared, the drive for family planning became much more action-oriented being directed at the professional medical and public health personnel. Articles on the subject in professional journals increased in number, and medical conferences for obstetricians, surgeons, medical administrators, experienced practitioners of traditional Chinese medicine and other medical personnel covered such topics as the effectiveness of the intra-uterine contraceptive device (I U D) and improvements in artificial abortion techniques and sterilization methods. Similar meetings at the lower administrative levels (*hsien* and commune) included discussions of the practical problems involved in working with the peasants. Medical seminars not directed at birth control nevertheless usually included this subject on the agenda.

A most important role in the drive to limit Chinese fertility during this period was played by the mobile medical teams, composed of groups of urban medical personnel who were required to spend a certain part of the year attending to the medical needs of the rural population. Among the duties specifically assigned to the teams, which increased to over 1,000 by 1966, was the mission to 'publicize the meaning of planned parenthood among the peasants and propagate the knowledge about birth control'. To accomplish this task members of the team conducted propaganda meetings, set up exhibitions, showed films and organized 'personal testimony' meetings at which peasant women who were using IUDs or other types of contraceptives described their reactions – favourable, of course.

With the advent of the Cultural Revolution China discontinued practically all publications and the few that continued were much too pre-occupied with political diatribes even to mention the subject of population. After some initial confusion on the part of the Red Guards as to whether birth control was 'revisionist', it was finally resolved to be a Maoist idea and family planning activities initiated in the countryside during the previous years were not disturbed. As a matter of fact, the thousands of additional medical personnel who were permanently moved out of the cities during and after the Cultural Revolution must have augmented the effort in the rural areas. Moreover, as in the case of mobile medical teams, specifically mentioned among the duties of the 'barefoot doctors' – the thousands of peasants who were given a modicum of medical training and sent out among the masses – was the propagation of birth control. This is verified by Edgar Snow who, after his 1970 visit, reported that 'barefoot doctors' are also 'bearers of China's effective birth control pills now in widespread use even in rural areas'. The continuing drive for family planning in the urban areas was evident from a January 1970 broadcast that initiated a 'shock week' campaign for birth control with the announcement that 'Vigorous efforts should be made to propagate widely birth control and late marriage . . . This task must be carried out in a penetrating and meticulous manner so that it will reach every household and be practised by each individual.'

Reactions and results
What effect did all this action, and at times inaction, have on China's birth rate ? Let us start from the beginning. Trying to convince an overwhelmingly rural, poorly motivated, superstitious population that they should delay marriage and make an effort to limit their number of offspring was not an easy undertaking. The difficulty was accentuated by the already mentioned traditional Chinese attitude in favour of large families. As an outgrowth of Confucian teachings and veneration of ancestors and because of the very practical need for additional family labour, there existed an overwhelming desire to beget sons. Despite the intensity of the 1956–7 campaign to further birth control, its impact was minimal and probably well summarized in a letter that appeared in a local newspaper in 1957: 'Contraceptive propaganda has not penetrated into the countryside and the use of the various kinds of contraceptive methods is mostly limited to the workers in the government agencies.' Other items that appeared in Chinese publications maintained

that 'the campaign has been ineffective in the rural areas, owing to ignorance, poor presentation, fears, superstitions and various mental obstacles'.

In addition to the problems of motivation and education, there were also the physical and economic problems of supplying hundreds of millions of persons in the reproductive ages with the necessary paraphernalia for effective birth control. In February 1958 one newspaper admitted in an editorial that the total supply of contraceptives in China was sufficient to meet the needs of only 2·2 per cent of all persons in the reproductive ages. In other words, even had the Chinese population accepted birth control in the decade of the 1950s, given the country's economic priorities, China simply could not have provided the people with adequate quantities of contraceptives.

Thus the fairly extensive efforts to curb Chinese fertility in the 1950s probably had little effect in the rural areas and only marginal success in the cities of China. As a matter of fact it has even been suggested that there was an increase in the birth rate following the Communist takeover. Because parental consent was no longer necessary, because women were assured that they had equal rights and no longer were dependent on either the father or the husband, and because economic security eliminated economic constraints, the marriage rate theoretically could have increased. Actually, however, there is much evidence that traditional values and customs in China are not put aside that quickly and that easily. It takes more than the mere proclamation of a new Marriage Law for a Chinese girl to practise this strange, new emancipation. As late as 1970 the Communists felt it necessary to carry a warning in the press: 'At present, the class enemies are still making use of the ghost of the doctrines of Confucius and Mencius and lingering pernicious influence of Liu Shao-ch'i's counterrevolutionary revisionist line [and] engage in the buying-and-selling type of matrimony . . .' Perhaps a local phenomenon, but it still seems doubtful that the new freedoms resulted in any immediate increase in marriage and fertility among the Chinese women.

Whereas during the 1950s the birth control campaign achieved only limited results, it seems very probable that during the following ten years – the decade of the sixties – the Chinese managed to start a gradual downward trend in the country's fertility. Considering all the difficulties earlier described, how is it possible to suggest such a change in so short a time?

The Chinese Communists have always seen the family – the traditional social unit in China, based on the Confucian principles of filial piety and brotherly love – as a major obstacle to the thoroughgoing establishment of communism in China. The efforts to redirect loyalties from family to the leadership in Peking have proceeded primarily on three fronts. First, through the promulgation of the Marriage Law and the 'emancipation' of women; second, through the indoctrination and education of children and youth; and third, through the collectivization and subsequent communization of agriculture. Much has been written about these policies. Although she may have left her heart at home, the 'liberated' housewife became an important unit of labour in the field and factory. Trained from infancy in the sanctity of Mao's thought, children were presumably encouraged to indoctrinate their parents, to inform on them and denounce any deviation from Maoist principles, singing that 'Dear are our parents, but dearer still is Chairman Mao'. Despite the propaganda and the creation of communes, which were originally intended to replace many of the family functions, the family continues to exist and the changes in the family structure have not been as great as party leaders desired. Even the *People's Daily* had to admit reluctantly in 1963 that 'owing to many historical reasons, the old way of thinking and old habits in marriage and family life are more difficult to eradicate than old customs in any other field'. Since then, the Cultural Revolution placed additional strains on the Chinese family. Many of the actions of the Red Guards were directed specifically at traditional filial piety, which implies both love and respect of the child for his parents. The deportation of millions of youth from Chinese cities was certainly not intended to perpetuate familial relationships, but because of the reported opposition to this separation on the part of the affected youth and parents it may be wrong to assume that this policy resulted in family bonds being permanently broken. Furthermore, rural families were not affected by this shift.

And yet, in this very changed society, the family changed too. Not so much because several generations no longer live under one roof under one family head, and not because a male child is no longer considered to be a form of old-age insurance, and not because there is less attachment and love – the family has changed because the social and economic organization of society has changed and with it the thinking of the young people. These conditions now point to the probability of fertility controls and their acceptance.

It is, of course, most important to reach the nation's youth who are potentially the most fertile group. In China, people under thirty constitute approximately two-thirds of the population and, since by the middle and late 1960s they had spent most of their young adulthood under the Communists, they are also the most thoroughly indoctrinated. During those years China made significant strides in providing the vast majority of the youth with at least a primary level education, so that most of the people in the young reproductive ages can no longer be considered illiterate. China is poor but not indigent. Some bad crop years notwithstanding, improved food distribution procedures have resulted in an absence of even regional starvation. A limited number of consumer goods is now more widely available. For better or for worse, political indoctrination and mandatory study of the thoughts of Mao have served to avert the intense dejection and desperation so prevalent among many people of underdeveloped countries. The young people of China have been saturated with government policies that denigrate family, cultural traditions and domesticity, but uphold service and sacrifice for motherland and socialist conformity – conformity so traditional in Chinese society. Because early marriage and numerous children are un-Maoist and reactionary, there now seems to be a stigma attached to having large families. Given the climate of opinion wherein small families are part of a patriotic duty, the youth might well be willing to postpone marriage and to accept and practise some form of birth control within the marriage relationship.

Relevant here are the activities (or inactivities) of the Red Guards during the Cultural Revolution. Despite some speculation to the contrary, China is one of the few countries in which millions of teenaged boys and girls can travel, demonstrate and sleep under the same roof without affecting the country's birth rate. In pre-Communist China, premarital sexual intercourse was regarded as extremely reprehensible, and chastity held a high place on the list of womanly virtues. This is one of the traditions of old China accepted and nurtured by the Communists and the 'liberation' of Chinese women does not extend to the endorsement of free love. All evidence suggests that China's youth continue to pursue the puritanical sexual mores of the past. There was truly little need for the slogan: 'Making love is a mental disease which wastes time and energy.'

Just in case the drive to sublimate the sex urge needed reinforcement, the media, particularly the publications catering to women and youth,

included articles encouraging family planning and the use of contraceptives. The 'letter to the editors' format, a particularly popular way
of communicating current social attitudes, was frequently used. For
example, a published letter from a young wife asked whether it is true
that contraception may induce 'sexual discord' and is 'harmful to bodily
health'. To this question, which was intended to reflect the concern of
many young people in China, the editor responded categorically that
one must 'refrain from believing in hearsay or offhand assertions'. In
great detail he then pointed out that contraception 'neither affects the
love one has for the other nor the normal sexual life of the husband and
wife' and that only persons who are 'lacking rudimentary knowledge of
physiology and personal hygiene' would suggest that the use of contraceptives is unhealthy. The conclusion: 'You should dispel your mis-
givings and worries, and persist in the practice of contraception until
you have achieved the object of planned childbirth.'

To be effective this gentle persuasion had to go hand-in-hand with
readily available means for family planning, and contraceptives such as
condoms, pills, foams, jellies, diaphragms and especially intra-uterine
devices were made more readily available throughout the countryside
in the 1960s. Perhaps of special significance was the increased use of
IUDs which have apparently become progressively more acceptable
from the point of view of the woman and of the medical personnel. The
IUD may not yet be entirely suitable for advanced Western countries,
but because they are inexpensive, because they can be inserted by
specially trained personnel with limited medical backgrounds, they are
extremely well suited for China. Chinese medical journals have reported numerous experiments with the IUD, and the *Chinese Journal of
Gynaecology and Obstetrics* stated in 1965 that the stainless steel contraceptive rings are popularly recommended in all the large cities of the
nation and welcomed by the masses.

Oral contraceptives seem to be as ancient as China itself, albeit they
are often difficult to distinguish from potions devised to induce abortion.
In his *Medical History of Contraception*, Norman Hines quotes from
the most ancient medical work in the Chinese language, put together
several centuries before the birth of Christ: '*Shui yin* tastes bitter, is of
cold nature, and contains poison. It is a specific for ulcers, white itching
sores on the scalp, will kill parasitical worms in the skin and flesh,
cause abortion and cure fevers . . .' Another ancient prescription is as
follows: 'Take a square foot or more sheet of paper on which silkworm

eggs have been hatched, burn to an ash and pulverize. After childbirth mix this in liquor and take. Those with impoverished blood will not again become pregnant for the rest of their lives.' Prescriptions such as these were passed on through the centuries, not only in medical books but also by word of mouth, from one practitioner of herb medicine to the next. As recently as 1956, a herbalist; who was also Deputy to the National People's Congress, suggested in all seriousness the following remedy that was quickly picked up by the sceptical world press: 'Fresh tadpoles coming out in the spring should be washed clean in cold well water, and swallowed whole three or four days after menstruation. If a woman swallows fourteen live tadpoles on the first day and ten more on the following day, she will not conceive for five years . . .'

Birth control pills, so popular in the West, are a relatively new phenomenon in China. Although Chinese medical journals have reported considerable research in the field of oral contraception, the limited supply and excessive cost hampered mass acceptance and usage of this new drug. More recent visitors to the People's Republic, however, have reported seeing prominent displays of oral contraceptive pills which they claim are in abundant supply in China's major cities. Given the necessary priority China's pharmaceutical industry is certainly now capable of producing these pills in such quantities as to affect China's birth rate. The remaining questions, of course, are whether there is this priority and whether the Chinese women – particularly in the rural areas – will adopt this method of birth control. Present indications are that the answer to this question must be made in the affirmative. According to Edgar Snow, who made a special effort to look into these questions during his trip to China in 1970, the developments in oral contraception have been dramatic during the past few years: the pills are manufactured in billions, distributed free of charge and are widely accepted by the Chinese women. This is confirmed by the fact that a recently published handbook for the ubiquitous 'barefoot doctors' includes details on the use and distribution of oral contraceptives to the women in the villages.

Abortion in China has never faced the moral or legal obstacles prevalent in the West. Nevertheless, although the prerequisites imposed by the regime in the 1950s were relatively loose and could be easily met by women anxious to terminate pregnancy, the lack of facilities and trained personnel made discussions relating to abortions for the most part theoretical in nature. Since then the number of induced abortions has increased significantly. In the mid-1960s numerous articles in medical journals detailed abortion procedures and reported statistical data culled from the experiences of individual doctors or medical institut.ons. The Chinese are also experimenting with simple methods and producing uncomplicated 'gadgets' that can be used by lower medical personnel in performing abortions in the rural areas. There is no way to estimate the incidence of abortion in the country, but as in Japan abortion will probably play an important role in reducing China's birth rate.

Sterilization has never been vigorously promoted in the People's Republic. Although it is usually the female who is most anxious to take the necessary measures to limit the family, the vasectomy, or male sterilization, is the easier and cheaper operation. Here, however, the desire to limit the number of births runs head-on both into the universal fear of surgery and into the difficulty of convincing the average male, be he Chinese or not, that vasectomy is not castration and that he will not experience any loss of sexuality. Finally, there is also the problem, as with abortion, of a shortage of hospital facilities and medical personnel to perform these operations. Despite these obstacles, sterilization has not been ignored. Articles encouraging it and publicizing the cases of individuals who have undergone these operations periodically appear in newspapers and especially in women's magazines. In the 1950s sterilization was a relatively limited urban phenomenon. Although since then the incidence of sterilization has been increasing rapidly, in all probability it is still an insignificant factor in reducing Chinese fertility.

With the above discussion as a backdrop, what then is the current Chinese birth rate? The figures can be little more than informed guesses, but it would seem that the crude birth rate of some 43 per 1,000 total population just prior to 1949 began to decrease slowly midway through the fifties to reach about 38 per 1,000 at the end of the first decade of Communist rule and about 32 per 1,000 at the end of the second.

If the above estimates are anywhere close to being realistic, this drop in the birth rate represents a tremendous achievement for a country that, for all practical purposes, is still underdeveloped. Despite continuing efforts by the regime and probably greater acceptance of family planning on the part of the population, the decrease in the crude birth rate, though likely to continue, will be at a slower rate. The reason for this is a fairly sharp and early decline in Chinese mortality which occurred under the new regime, resulting in an increase in the number

D

of surviving children and, starting with the late 1960s, in considerably larger cohorts of women entering the reproductive ages. Since the birth rate is a gross figure calculated in relation to the country's total population, the increased rate of survival among babies anc children would first tend to depress the birth rate (total population growing more rapidly than population in reproductive ages), and as the young people reach reproductive ages (1970s), it would increase the birth rate. In simpler words, although the average number of children per woman may decrease slightly, there will be a larger proportion of these women capable of having children. All in all, China would probably be doing extremely well if she could drop the birth rate to, say, 20 to 25 per 1,000 by the year 1980.

Mortality

Presumably on the basis of sample reporting areas, as in the case of the birth rate, the Chinese published a death rate in conjunction with the 1953 census activity of 17 per 1,000 total population – a rate that seems much too low for the conditions that prevailed in China during that time period. To evaluate that figure and to consider the trends in mortality since then, it is necessary briefly to consider Chinese policies and practices in medicine and public health during the past twenty years.

Advances in public health

As the reader knows, the Communists inherited serious health problems when they assumed control, but they placed a high priority on the improvement of the country's health conditions. Lacking personnel and facilities for treatment of illnesses, they emphasized preventive medicine and sanitation. Millions of people were vaccinated and mass campaigns were instituted to improve environmental sanitation and to encourage personal hygiene. Millions of people (including children and the aged) were mobilized to participate in the well-publicized campaign to exterminate the 'four pests' – mosquitoes, flies, rats and sparrows – and, in general, to clean up the cities and the countryside. With these programmes the government did succeed in greatly reducing the occurrence of major infectious and parasitic diseases.

Alongside improvements in environmental sanitation and personal hygiene came the efforts to increase medical facilities such as clinics, hospitals and sanatoriums, to accelerate the training of medical personnel and to recast and enhance their traditionally low image. In pre-Communist China, the great majority of the 20,000 or so doctors practising Western medicine in the country were trained abroad in Europe, the United States or Japan. But under the Mao regime, higher education in medicine kept pace with the rapid growth of education in general and despite some fluctuations in enrolment and educational philosophy, particularly during the Great Leap Forward period, it is estimated that by the end of 1966 there were approximately 200,000 persons in the People's Republic with completed higher medical education.

More important, however, in terms of the country's health was the new emphasis placed on secondary medical education and, below that, on a variety of short-term medical training courses for both full-time and part-time medical and public health workers. Many of the students in these courses were recruited from the countryside, trained in nearby commune medical centres and, upon completion of their training, returned to their native villages. Obviously with their limited training they were unable to perform major surgery, for example, but they could provide adequate medical care for the majority of the population and in this way overcome a problem faced by other developing countries – the difficulty of providing the most basic medical services to their rural population.

During the mid 1960s, as a first stage in spreading medical aid to the most remote corners of rural China, Peking introduced mobile medical teams (which included the better-qualified medical personnel) to tend the more serious cases during periodic visits to the communes. The second step was to transfer large numbers of doctors and other medical personnel from the cities to the countryside on a more permanent basis. And finally they instituted the already-mentioned system of politically pure 'barefoot doctors' who were trained to provide first aid, give inoculations and carry out simple health procedures, and to do all these tasks while actively involved in the production of their work teams.

Any discussions of medical manpower in China must also include the role of traditional Chinese medicine, an empirical healing art based on thousands of years of practical experience. After an initial tug-of-war between medical and political leaders, the latter predictably won and the Chinese made an all-out effort to give traditional medicine equal status with Western medicine. In Peking's view traditional medicine had many outstanding advantages. The training of traditional practitioners – 'native doctors' – was much quicker and easier since it relied on learning from elders and 'practising while learning'. However, to ensure equal status for both Western and Chinese medicine, the regime had not only to build up the validity of herb medicine but at the same time to deprecate modern medical practices. For this purpose, courses in traditional medicine were introduced in all medical schools, physicians practising Western medicine were required to take special courses in traditional medicine, and both types of doctors found themselves working side by side in hospitals and clinics throughout the country.

Western medical opinion about Chinese traditional medicine differs. Some believe it to be little more than black magic; others feel that the thousands of herbs and drug potions and the healing arts of acupuncture, moxibustion, massage and breathing therapy have lasted all these years because of their empirical value. Acupuncture, whose practitioners claim that disease can be cured by the insertion of stainless steel needles into specified parts of the body, has gained ground as a mass treatment. Chinese press and radio have praised acupuncture and moxibustion – a related practice of burning cones of dried herbs on the needle points – for having cured ailments ranging from stomach trouble to blindness by restoring equilibrium in the human body. American doctors who recently visited the People's Republic were particularly impressed with acupuncture anaesthesia, which makes major surgery possible simply by inserting needles into certain points on the limbs, ears, nose or face and stimulating these needles either manually or electrically. It is not necessary to fathom the mystery of acupuncture to appreciate the importance of people feeling that someone cares, and that something is being done about their particular ailment, whether the prescription is successful or not. By establishing the Academy of Traditional Chinese Medicine in 1955 and decreeing equal status between Western and traditional medicine three years later, the Chinese immediately increased their pool of medical personnel by over 500,000 and made it possible to continue training additional practitioners in a 'quick, good, cheap' manner.

Better health, new policies
To consider the effects of improved health conditions in China on the country's mortality trends, it is necessary to juxtapose the health

facilities and manpower with the political and economic fluctuations that cyclically affect the life (and death) of the Chinese people.

In countries with high death rates the principal causes are infectious and epidemic diseases and extremely high infant and child mortality – causes which readily respond to health measures of the type introduced by the Communists. Probably as early as 1951, China's death rate, which is estimated to have been in the low thirties just prior to the Communist takeover, started its downward trend. It is inconceivable that it would have dropped to anywhere near the 17 per 1,000 reported for 1953, but it did continue to decline during the middle 1950s until the introduction of the Great Leap Forward in 1958 when it may have been as low as 22 per 1,000. The extended working hours, long political indoctrination sessions and lack of sleep and rest that were so characteristic of the frantic production drive during the Great Leap made millions of workers more susceptible to sickness and disease. Furthermore, of particular significance in terms of health were the conditions at the numerous construction projects, which engaged scores of millions of people and in which many of the most basic sanitary measures were absent. Hard labour, exposure, dirt, disease and a poor diet were bound to take their toll and undoubtedly negated the favourable effects of the continuing expansion of medical facilities.

During the next three years conditions in China deteriorated rapidly. The degree of severity of the hard years following the Great Leap on the life and death of the Chinese people is yet another area of speculation. Although the serious reduction in the production of food crops between 1959 and 1961 and the food shortages that followed are part of the known record, the reports of widespread famine by refugees who entered Hong Kong during these years were probably exaggerated. Nevertheless, the death rate undoubtedly increased resulting in an excess mortality of perhaps five to seven million persons. By 1962 mortality probably had resumed its downward trend and by the middle of the decade may have again reached the level of before the Great Leap – estimated at about 22 per 1,000. During the Cultural Revolution the conditions in many parts of China were again unfavourable, but because most of the turmoil and reported increases in the incidence of some diseases were limited to the urban areas, there was probably only a slight pause in the continuing decline in mortality. It is estimated that by 1970 China finally reached the figure of 17 per 1,000, reported seventeen years earlier.

Barring disasters, natural or man-made, China's mortality should continue downward, but very slowly. The decline of mortality in China was achieved primarily through the introduction of environmental sanitation which tended to decrease vulnerability to death, preventive medicine in the form of inoculations and injections, and a large increase in the number of public health facilities and personnel. A drop in the death rate to levels found in more advanced countries is not likely for some time to come. China will continue to be overwhelmingly rural and the hard work and disabling accidents that occur in traditional agriculture are not conducive to longevity. Although there is an increasing use of chemical fertilizers in agriculture, raw manure will still be applied. Consequently, elimination of certain diseases (particularly of the digestive tract) is virtually impossible. In the long run, a continuing drop in the level of mortality could only be achieved through an improvement in the quality of medical attention provided to the people – with more emphasis on the curative rather than the preventative approach. With the post-Cultural Revolution emphasis on 'barefoot doctors' and traditional Chinese medicine, and with the drastically shortened curriculum for new medical personnel, medical care will continue to be more accessible to all, but its quality is not likely to show great improvement. Furthermore, if Peking decides to change the emphasis back to Western medicine, it will still be decades before well-trained medical people become available in large enough numbers to provide the Chinese peasants with up-to-date medical care. It is very possible, however, that this is not a course China will choose in the near future: the investment of scarce capital in medical training would, concomitantly, increase the rate of population growth. Whether consciously or subconsciously, the leaders in Peking may very well feel that the country has reached a satisfactory balance, for it is providing quite adequate health care for all the people and at the same time is limiting population growth by maintaining what could be considered a reasonable level of mortality.

Natural increase, present size and prospects

Having pondered the population data reported by the Chinese themselves and having speculated on the trends in China's vital rates, we arrive face to face with the inevitable question: just what is the popula-

Table 3: Selected population estimates for the People's Republic of China (population in thousands)

year	US Bureau of the Census[1]		United Nations[2] (medium variant)		Orleans[3]	
	number	average annual growth rate	number	average annual growth rate	number	average annual growth rate
1960	718,004		—		655,000	
		1·8		—		1·4
1965	782,555		695,000		701,000	
		2·3		1·8		1·5
1970	871,035		759,619		753,000	
		2·1		1·7		1·7
1975	962,480		825,821		818,000	
		2·0		1·6		1·7
1980	1,060,695		893,900		887,000	

[1] J. S. Aird, *Estimates and Projections of the Population of Mainland China: 1953–86*, US Bureau of the Census, Series P-91, No. 17 (Washington: 1968). Stagnation model, five per cent undercount – the series preferred by Aird.

[2] *World Population Prospects, 1965–85 as Assessed in 1968*, United Nations, Population Division, Working Paper No. 30 (December 1969). This is not an official document of the United Nations, but rather an internal working paper for informational and consultative purposes.

[3] These estimates are based on the following general assumptions: (1) The reported rates of natural increase between 1953 and 1958 were too high, primarily because of an unrealistically low death rate; (2) starting with the late 1950s, the birth rate began on a very gradual and hesitant downward trend – a trend that will continue during the 1970s; and (3) despite some fluctuations during the 1950s and 1960s, the overall downward trend of the death rate will also continue, but very slowly. For a detailed discussion and assumed annual vital rates, see L. A. Orleans, 'Propheteering: The Population of Communist China', *Current Scene*, Vol. VII, No. 24 (Hong Kong: 1969).

tion of the People's Republic? If the Chinese themselves have apparently lost count of their vast population – and they do not seem to show great concern about the absence of demographic statistics – shouldn't it be sufficient for the rest of us to acknowledge that China has by far the largest population of any country and leave it at that? Perhaps. But our penchant for precision, our fascination with other sides of Chinese economic, social and political developments, our curiosity and delight in playing academic guessing games, all require something 'more scientific', something that at least suggests authority and authenticity.

To satisfy these needs, individuals and institutions in many countries have attempted to estimate China's total population. The approaches range from outright guesses to application of the most sophisticated demographic techniques. The validity of all the estimates, however, rests in the eyes of the beholder, and *caveat emptor* hides behind every figure. Nevertheless, the most authoritative and the most widely used figures are those published by the US Bureau of the Census and by the United Nations Population Division. It is interesting to note that the Soviet Union has never published an original estimate of China's population, relying on the all-purpose round figures used by Peking or on Western estimates. Although both the US Bureau of the Census and the United Nations have used a variety of assumptions and range of estimates, table 3 presents what can be considered as their best estimates – the 'medium variant' – and compares them with the author's calculations. The diversity of the figures speaks for itself.

Is it reasonable to expect that given a modicum of stability in China over the next few years, Peking will attempt another national census? At this time it seems to be an unlikely prospect. Because of the complexity and cost of such an effort and because China's national plans and policies are not tied to statistical precision, she will probably continue to make do with her current registration system and whatever approximations Peking's oracles can muster. But even if China were to attempt a more formal count of her population, the published figures would only heighten speculation and controversy. After all, despite adequate funds, the latest computers, experienced staff and all the other prerequisites for an accurate count, the 1960 census of the United States had an error of more than three per cent – increasing to seventeen per cent among the non-white young males. Given the persistent nature of the handicaps discussed in this chapter, it is difficult to foresee a time when the size of China's population will not be in dispute.

and later as capitals of various feudal states, as fortresses during periods of expansion and colonization, and finally as administrative centres that symbolized authority and power of the Chinese emperors. Character- istically, Chinese cities were established first and foremost as political and cultural centres that also functioned as nodes for trade and market- ing; the reverse order generally prevailed in the Western world. In those days cities were very much a part of the surrounding countryside, and the life-style of their residents did not show any characteristic differences from the rural population. With rare exceptions, these administrative centres were the largest cities within the area they con- trolled, and curiously most of them not only managed to survive centuries of turmoil and calamities but continue even now to maintain a leading political and economic role in their region.

Because throughout most of her history China has been an inward- looking country, both politically and with regard to trade, most of her important urban centres developed in the interior. It was not until the mid-nineteenth century that traders from the West established signifi- cant trading bases along the Chinese coastline, influenced the growth of those port cities which eventually developed into the country's economic, financial and educational centres, and opened the often reluctant gates to modernization – Western style. In the twentieth cen- tury, and particularly during the 1920s and 1930s, industrial growth reached China's larger cities and caused a rapid influx of migrants, either from surrounding rural areas or from the more distant provinces, as was the case in Manchuria which drew hundreds of thousands of people from north China. Most of these migrants consisted of young males. Although much of this migration was temporary or seasonal in nature, there was a constant excess of males and it was characteristic that Chinese cities of this period had a very high male-sex ratio. Never- theless, because of traditional values and because many of the males who came to find employment in the cities left their families in the villages, a close link continued to exist between large segments of the urban population and their ancestral rural home.

Although some scattered figures for individual cities can be found in historical materials, there are virtually no estimates of the size of the urban population. Infrequent Chinese and Western estimates during the Republic period (1911–49) appear to be unrelated, show no chrono- logical trend, and are more confusing than revealing. Absolute figures vary from 100 to 150 million; as a proportion of total population, estimates vary from about twenty to thirty per cent; surprisingly some of the largest discrepancies are found in guesses as to the number of urban settlements that existed in the country.

Data and definitions

In any discussion of size and growth of the Chinese cities, the 1953 census figure for the urban population once again without question provides the only acceptable base.

The census reported an urban population of 77, 257, 282 or 13·26 per cent of the total population – probably the lowest estimate of this century, both in absolute figures and as per cent of total. The procedures and problems discussed earlier relating to the 1953 census and total populations are, for the most part, equally as pertinent to the urban population. An additional concern however, which undoubtedly caused considerable confusion in 1953 and since then, is that of defining urban population.

There are no international criteria for what is 'urban' and great variations exist from one country to the next. In general, such factors as size of settlement, its administrative significance and the proportion of its population engaged in nonagricultural pursuits are taken into consideration. Although undoubtedly some guidelines must have been provided to the local census officials in China, no specific standards defining urban population were ever published. More important, no matter what criteria might have been suggested in 1953, they would have been extremely difficult if not impossible to apply with any degree of accuracy. China has many large settlements which would meet size requirements in most countries, but are nevertheless predominantly agricultural in nature. If occupational criteria were to be used, it is most unlikely that data would be available to enable classification of individual settlements as urban or rural. Nor could such information be obtained from the census itself, since no question was asked relating to occupation. Most towns contain a certain proportion of people engaged in farming; were they included or excluded from the urban population? Possibly the reason that the 1953 urban population figure was at least thirty million lower than the pre-Communist estimates was the exclusion of agricultural population living within the city limits. In many cities this segment of the population could account for as much as ten to twenty per cent of its total population. In settlements that were clearly urban, the problem was to define their administrative boundaries, which at best would not be very precise and at worst would be non-existent. Discrepancies due to imprecise city lines would probably increase with the size of the city and could be quite significant for

Table 4: Number of urban places and the urban population by size of place: June 1953
(population in thousands)

size of place	number of urban places	urban population number	urban population per cent
1,000,000 or more	9	21,020	27·2
500,000 to 999,999	16	11,279	14·6
200,000 to 499,999	28	8,492	11·0
100,000 to 199,999	49	7,201	9·3
50,000 to 99,999	71	5,497	7·1
20,000 to 49,999	247		
2,000 to 19,999	4,228	23,768	30·8
1,000 to 1,999	727		
Less than 1,000	193		
Total	5,568	77,257	100·0

Source: Adapted from: M. B. Ullman, Cities of Mainland China 1953 and 1958, US Bureau of the Census (August 1961). The reported population of cities is known to include a certain proportion of rural population. All cities over and 62 cities under 100,000 were designated as municipalities which, because of their administrative, industrial, or commercial significance, are independent administrative units.

densely populated areas. Nevertheless on the basis of the 1953 census the Chinese reported a precise total of 5,568 urban places (see table 4), including many county seats which 'are far from modern cities and close to villages'.

It was not until November 1955 that the State Council attempted to define 'urban' and instructed the Ministry of Interior to develop a guide on urban and urban-type areas. A definition apparently was agreed upon; an area would be defined as urban if it met any one of these three criteria: (a) seat of municipal people's committee or people's committee

Table 5: Cities of 500,000 or more inhabitants: 1953

city	province	population (*in thousands*)
Shanghai	Kiangsu	6,204·4
Peking	Hopei	2,768·1
Tientsin	Hopei	2,693·8
Shen-yang (Mukden)	Liaoning	2,299·9
Chungking	Szechwan	1,772·5
Kuang-chou (Canton)	Kwangtung	1,598·9
Wu-han	Hupei	1,427·3
Harbin	Heilungkiang	1,163·0
Nanking	Kiangsu	1,091·6
Tsingtao	Shantung	916·8
Ch'eng-tu	Szechwan	856·7
Ch'ang-ch'un	Kiangsu	855·2
Hsi-an (Sian)	Shensi	787·3
Ta-lien (Dairen)	Liaoning	766·4
T'ai-yuan	Shansi	720·7
K'un-ming	Yunnan	698·9
Hang-chou (Hangchow)	Chekiang	696·6
T'ang-shan	Hopei	693·3
Chi-nan (Tsinan)	Shangtung	680·1
Fu-shun	Liaoning	678·6
Ch'ang-sha	Hunan	650·6
Cheng-chou	Honan	594·7
Wu-hsi	Kiangsu	581·5
Fu-chou (Foochow)	Fukien	553·0
An-shan	Liaoning	548·9

Source: A. G. Shiger, *Administrativno-Territorial'noye Deleniye Zarubezhnykh Stran* (Moskva: 1957).

above the *hsien* (county) level; (b) a minimum resident population of 2,000, at least fifty per cent of which is nonagricultural; and (c) a resident population of between 1,000 and 2,000, seventy-five per cent of which is nonagricultural. Unfortunately, again, there is no way of determining to what extent this definition prevailed or, for that matter, whether, assuming the best of intentions (which was not always the case), data were available to enable application of the criteria.

Despite the fact that no urban population series was published for the first seven years of Communist control, in June 1957 a detailed analysis of the urban–rural distribution of the population of China appeared in the official publication of the State Statistical Bureau (see table 6).

Table 6: Size and rate of growth of the urban population of China

end of year	total population	urban population	per cent urban	per cent of increase over preceding year
	in thousands			
1949	541,670	57,650	10·60	—
1950	551,960	61,690	11·12	7·00
1951	563,000	66,320	11·78	7·50
1952	574,820	71,630	12·46	8·00
1953	587,960	77,670	13·21	8·43
1954	601,720	81,550	13·55	4·99
1955	614,650	82,850	13·48	1·59
1956	627,800	89,150	14·20	7·60

Source: T'ung-chi kung-tso (Statistical Work), No. 11 (1957).

At first glance the figures look impressive and reasonable, but a closer analysis of the statistics and of the accompanying text raises a number of questions which tend to support the doubts about Peking's ability to produce accurate figures of the country's population. According to *Statistical Work*, 'The figures for the urban population for 1949, 1950 and 1951 are estimates based on the rate of population increase in cities and towns in the north-west and north-east.' Not only are these two regions not representative of China as a whole, but they contain less than a third of the country's total population. Furthermore, the rates of increase for these years are too regular (7·00, 7·50 and 8·00) and were probably arrived at arbitrarily – working backwards from the 1953 census population.

'The figures for 1954 and 1955 are based on the reports of provinces and municipalities.' Since by the end of 1955 the registration system was, according to Chinese reports, still in the process of being established, how accurate could the data be on which the estimates were based? Similarly, the 1956 urban rate of growth was stated to be derived from reports of only fourteen provinces and three municipalities – a somewhat incomplete basis for estimating the growth of the country's urban population.

Unquestionably, the reported figures (in table 6) are little more than approximations. But it should quickly be added that they still constitute our only basis for estimating urban population. During the next couple of years only a few additional figures were published before all urban estimates got completely washed away by the continuous ebb and flow of the migrants in and out of the cities of China.

Trends in urban migration

During the previous fifty years, millions of people who came in search of employment in China's new industries and growing commerce had to settle in vast slum areas of makeshift housing. The problem was further aggravated by decades of political instability and turmoil and by almost ten years of the Sino-Japanese War. During this war, tens of millions of people left the large cities that were in the path of the Japanese advance, while other millions were left homeless through widespread bombings and fires which in some cases almost completely destroyed the cities. Although some reconstruction had taken place by 1949, large districts of dilapidated housing and a variety of shelters of indigenous material and scrap, made by impoverished but resourceful Chinese, were to be found in war-damaged cities as well as in those cities not directly affected by the conflict.

During most of the 1950s the flow of peasants towards the cities was greatly accelerated. The two most powerful forces to promote urban growth in the People's Republic have been the pull exerted by industrialization in the cities and the push applied by the sometimes ruthlessly enforced collectivization, and later communalization, of the countryside. Both forces working towards the same objective siphoned millions of peasants from the rural areas, prompting the Chinese newspapers and journals to describe the movement as a 'blind infiltration' of the cities. The traditional shortage of urban housing in China became particularly acute with the influx of these peasants.

Because of the serious housing problems and, additionally, the difficulties of feeding, schooling and finding work for the new wave of migrants, the new regime was quick to react. The first directive attempting to control farmers coming into the cities was issued in April 1953.

In March 1954, the Ministries of Internal Affairs and Labour issued a joint directive to 'dissuade farmers from pouring blindly into the cities'. It was obvious that directives alone would not suffice and the regime was soon forced to introduce other measures. By 1955 widespread efforts were made to round up the 'nonproductive elements' in the cities and return them to their villages while, at the same time, trying to institute and enforce much stricter controls over the 'senseless migration of rural population into the cities'. These new stringent rules among other things required all citizens to have certificates of employment or of acceptance from a school, or an official document from an urban agency for the administration of population registers, approving the move.

But these measures were able at best only to repress the growth. A Shanghai newspaper expressed great concern over the growth of that city's population from 5 million in 1950 to 6·2 million in 1953 to 7 million by the middle of 1955, of whom 'only 2·57 million actually participate in production or are related . . . to production'. To ameliorate this situation, during some six months of 1955 that city 'mobilized a total of 555,000 persons for return to the rural areas'. Nevertheless, as people were being moved out others apparently managed to enter, so that by the middle of 1956 the population of the city reportedly had increased by yet another half million. The desperate situation in Shanghai was repeated on a smaller scale in hundreds of towns and cities in China.

In 1957 the Chinese seemed to pursue their efforts even more vigorously to control and reduce the swelling urban population. The Ministry of Public Security intensified its controls over unauthorized migration, while at the same time hundreds of thousands of people were being 'persuaded' to 'go down' to the rural areas. The greatest emphasis was placed on reducing the ratio between administrative and productive personnel, particularly by reassigning government and party cadres and transferring recent primary and secondary school graduates to the rural areas. By early 1958 a million cadres and perhaps twice as many youths were reportedly moved out of the cities. How many of them remained in the countryside permanently is impossible to say, but due either to a return movement or to continued inefficiency of controls, the urban population continued to grow.

The next year, the year of the Great Leap Forward, a new wave of migrants flooded the cities – among them many of the cadres and students who had been transferred to rural areas just the previous year.

It is not known to what extent this was a 'natural' movement prompted by relaxed controls or even by Peking's desire to supplement the urban labour force, so seriously overextended and overworked during this period. Government spokesmen, however, repeatedly expressed the belief that an increase in production could be achieved by throwing additional manpower, steeped in revolutionary enthusiasm, into almost any activity. To mobilize this dormant energy Peking introduced the urban commune, a new social and economic base for the urban population. It was to create a new communal interdependence that would take the place of 'old fashioned' private life and at the same time involve the underemployed urban population in some form of productive effort. Almost immediately the urban communes ran into innumerable difficulties, from administrative and jurisdictional confusion to economic inefficiency of street industries and other collective work activities left primarily to women and children. Thus, the urban commune turned out to be both an economic and a social failure, fading away over a period of several years.

It was commonly reported (and usually accepted) that the urban population of China increased by some twenty million persons during the Great Leap, over a 1957 figure of almost ninety million. Some estimates of urban population in 1959 ran as high as 130 million. This urban increase was closely tied to just as fantastic an increase in the number of workers and employees (wage earners, most of whom are employed within the urban economy), from 24·5 million in 1957 to over 45 million by the end of 1958 (including workers in communal industries).

Although a spurt in the urban population during the Great Leap is not in question, a twenty-million increase in only one year must be rejected by common sense. Communist writings have made it patently clear how difficult, if not impossible, it was to absorb the rural migrants into the urban economy when they were coming at a rate of several million a year – admitting in 1956 that the urban economy can absorb only one million additional workers per year. Although after a relatively slow start the construction of residential housing accelerated during the First Five-Year Plan to almost twenty million square metres of housing per year and continued at a high pace through 1959, the available housing never caught up with the demand. An additional twenty million urban population could not possibly have been accommodated. The problem of feeding the urban population was already acute, as

E

was the burden on public transport, utilities, commercial establish-ments and other public services. Even if the cities could accommodate such a number, China did not have a pool of skilled or even semi-skilled labour that could be called on to support urban economic activities – and how many unskilled peasants could possibly be utilized productively? Obviously nowhere near twenty million.

On the other hand, if it is assumed that the twenty-million figure itself is not fictitious, explanations can be offered to justify such an increase in urban population without implying an actual migration of that magnitude. The increase in the number of workers and employees was achieved largely by putting to work millions of unproductive people who were already located in the urban areas and by reclassifying millions of other workers, such as the handicraftsmen, who were already active in the labour force but were not receiving wages from the state. Because the definition of 'urban' is based partly on the occupational composition of the labour force in a particular locality, such a reclassi-fication would have shifted many communities into the 'urban' category without any population movement at all.

The trend towards increasing local self-sufficiency in 1958 also contributed to the drastic increase in the urban population. Because it was desirable for municipalities to be self-sufficient and to have sources of food supply under their immediate jurisdictions, many of the large cities incorporated adjacent rural areas, and sometimes whole *hsien*. Thus the population of Shanghai increased from about seven to ten million during the Great Leap through the incorporation of ten *hsien*. During the same period, the population of Peking increased from four million to about six million when the area of the municipality was expanded from 4,700 to 17,000 square kilometres. According to a later report, of the 7·4 million people in the Peking municipality in 1963, 300,000 families engaged in agriculture. Unfortunately there were only a few instances where specific information was reported either on the expanded area or on what proportion of the added population was dependent on agriculture. For most of the cities reporting much larger population totals, there was no way to determine what part of the growth was due to migration, to natural increase or to the expansion of area within the jurisdiction. Nevertheless, if there was in fact a twenty-million increase in the urban population during 1958, factors other than migration were largely responsible and the increase therefore, to a large extent, was artificial.

The serious internal crisis which developed on the heels of the Great Leap, and the ensuing natural calamities, forced a complete revision of China's economic policies. The accent on agriculture instead of industry went hand-in-hand with renewed efforts to control and reduce the urban population. Many of the industrial enterprises in urban areas (particularly food processing and textile industries) were forced out of operation by the shortage of raw materials. Other enterprises were designated as uneconomic and closed down, the excess labour thus created being sent back to the rural areas. Every extra person in the city was said to be a burden on agriculture, for despite extended control over adjacent agricultural lands, large cities still had to import food-stuffs from more distant provinces, causing a considerable burden on the country's transportation system. Although the authorities probably were unable to transfer all the surplus urban manpower to the rural areas, 'the urban population was appropriately reduced'.

By 1962 China began to recover from the economic depression. Although emphasis continued to be on agriculture, light industry that was agriculture-related (such as fertilizer and farm equipment plants) also received priority. Despite Peking's expressed desire that in the immediate future 'the labour necessary for cities should be drawn primarily from the resources of labour in the cities' and attracted by the economic upswing, the workers who had been forced to return to the countryside during the previous few years began drifting back into the cities. Undoubtedly their number was supplemented by first-time migrants. At the same time reporting continued of many thousands of young urban 'intellectuals' being evacuated to the rural areas. Clashing head-on with the widespread and well-founded belief that only education can deliver the manual labourer from a lifetime of drudgery, the Party argued that: 'If all people of our country go to school to study and acquire culture and, after graduation, will not want to engage in productive labour . . . how can we get our food and clothing and how can society exist and develop?' The simultaneous flow of people in and out of the cities continued until the Cultural Revolution in 1966 but, on balance, China's urban population moved hand-in-hand with her ascending economy, showing a continuous growth during the middle 1960s.

During the first two years of the turbulent Cultural Revolution the country was much too concerned with immediate problems to concentrate on shifting people out of the cities. On the contrary, a good proportion of the many millions of Red Guards who wandered around the country and demonstrated in Tien-an-men Square in Peking came from the rural areas. After the regime finally decided to put a stop to their rampages, many Red Guards apparently took advantage of the confusion to remain in the cities from which they had been moved in previous years. This undetermined residual that remained in the urban areas precipitated an order that would severely punish the 'small number of youths who have disappeared, refused to report their real names and posts, disseminated rumours, deceived people, disturbed social security or destroyed state property'.

Efforts to return the Red Guards to their posts gradually expanded into the most intensive movement undertaken by Peking up to that time to move a significant proportion of the urban population – again primarily the youth – out of the cities. As in such previous campaigns, it reflected Mao's belief that China's salvation lies in the ultimate collapse of the barriers between the 'urban mandarins' and the impoverished rural masses, urging 'young intellectuals' leaving the cities to 'integrate with the peasants' for the purpose of 'making revolution'. It was also an opportunity to remove excess manpower from the factory and the government bureau and reduce the very prevalent 'featherbedding' practices while simultaneously easing the problem of feeding a large urban population. Heard during the period of particularly strained relations between China and the Soviet Union, other often cited reasons offered by Peking for the movement of youth to the countryside were for 'preparedness against war' and to increase self-sufficiency in case of an enemy invasion. Self-sufficiency was, in fact, an important goal, but it is hard to believe that through isolation China's fantasies produced an actual fear of an invasion. More likely it was another attempt to use an external threat as a means of fostering a new domestic policy intended to provide a method for the absorption of the rapidly growing manpower pool by introducing local industry into the countryside (see chapter 6).

What about the volume of this latest exodus? Naturally no comprehensive figures were reported, but Western estimates of the number of persons involved in this movement out of China's urban areas gradually increased in five-million increments from ten million to as high as twenty-five and thirty million. Although the significance of the migration should not be underestimated, it is still most problematical that the total number of people involved reached anywhere near twenty-five or thirty million. The Chinese press reported the departure of large numbers of bureaucrats and medical personnel, and some workers, but rarely did it mention family-type migration. Most of the propaganda was directed specifically at educated young Chinese (usually meaning anyone with at least a middle secondary education) but there are probably fewer than twenty-five million 'educated young Chinese' in the total urban population. Furthermore, it seems doubtful that the excess manpower in Chinese cities could have constituted only a third of the working force during a period when all indications pointed to a recuperative and even a growing period in the Chinese urban economy.

Looking at the migration from the rural side, it is likewise difficult to imagine how the villages could have physically, economically and psychologically absorbed twenty to thirty million youths even in the endless sea of peasants. Housing alone for so many people would have been a major obstacle. The concern was not only with the complaints of city youth who baulked at going to rural areas and their reported unhappiness with the harsh commune life they found there; it was also with the unhappiness of the peasants (already hard-pressed by State production quotas) suddenly faced with new mouths to feed. Most peasants apparently considered the new arrivals not as useful, productive labourers, but as still another burden to be carried by the rural comrades. One revolutionary committee of a production brigade commented on this problem with typical Cultural Revolution rhetoric: 'The forces of spontaneous capitalism in the rural areas are like a pool of slimy water which has not been cleaned away and is still giving off a terrible stench' – presumably a stench that will disappear after the proper 're-education' of everyone concerned.

A figure for the urban population?

Can all the speculation regarding trends be translated into specific estimates of the size of the urban population? Only in a tentative way. Despite reservations mentioned earlier with regard to the population series presented in table 6, there is no valid alternative to accepting the last figure of 89,150,000 as the urban population for year-end 1956. During the Great Leap the urban population may have reached a peak of 110 to 115 million. Despite a natural annual increase of some two per cent, it probably declined by a few million during 1960 and 1961, and then began another gradual period of growth. By the end of 1966 it may have reached 120 to 130 million, swelled temporarily by perhaps five million, and then dropped back again during the latest movement out of the cities. Lacking definitions as well as data can only result in extremely tenuous estimates, and yet, to gain some perspective, it is important to have some order of magnitude figure of the size of the urban population. It is therefore suggested that in January 1970 the urban population of China was 125 million, plus or minus five million.

The geographic distribution of the urban population is as difficult to ascertain as its size. The 1953 census results did not include the provincial distribution of the urban population, listing only those cities with over 100,000 people. Some scattered figures for smaller towns appeared during subsequent years, presumably quoting 1953 data. Table 7 presents an estimate of the provincial distribution of the urban population for mid 1953. Any current estimate as to this distribution would of necessity be so problematical as to make it virtually useless. Nevertheless, distribution of the urban population probably remained essentially the same, so that Kiangsu Province (including Shanghai) continues to have the largest urban population followed by Hopei Province (including Peking and Tientsin), while Liaoning undoubtedly remains the most urbanized province of China. If the 1953 to 1958 patterns of urban growth persisted, then some of the peripheral provinces which had the most rapid total population growth also experienced an urban growth above the national average. In the final analysis the Chinese Communists will find it extremely difficult (if not impossible) to change basically the existing urban patterns – despite some positive efforts devoted to the problem.

What of the future trends of China's urban population? It could normally be expected that urban growth would be directly proportional to industrial growth. Thus, lacking the necessary population figures, it should at least be possible to project industrial growth and correlate future urban growth to it. Not so in China. According to Mao, there is no direct correlation between industrialization and urbanization. The complementary policies of decentralization of industry and local self-sufficiency make sure of that.

Among the many advantages of developing industry in the countryside are the possibilities of utilizing available rural manpower while reducing procurement problems, investment in urban overhead, strain on the inadequate transport system and so forth. As for the inefficiency inherent in the type of decentralization currently practised by China,

Table 7: Provincial distribution of urban population: 1953
(population in thousands)

province	total	urban number	urban per cent of total
NE			
Heilungkiang	11,897	3,697	31·1
Kirin	11,290	3,274	29·0
Liaoning	20,566	8,648	42·0
N			
Shansi	14,314	1,846	12·9
Hopei	43,348	10,077	23·2
Shantung	48,877	3,356	6·9
Honan	44,215	2,889	6·5
C			
Hupei	27,790	2,388	8·6
Hunan	33,227	2,337	7·0
Kiangsi	16,773	1,269	7·2
E			
Kiangsu	47,137	13,733	29·1
Anhwei	30,663	2,046	6·7
Chekiang	22,866	2,234	9·8
SE			
Fukien	13,143	1,583	12·0
Kwangtung	36,740	4,494	12·2
Kwangsi	17,591	846	4·8
SW			
Kweichow	15,037	586	3·9
Yunnan	17,473	1,294	7·4
Szechwan	65,685	6,393	9·7
NW			
Sinkiang	4,874	526	10·8
Tsinghai	1,676	117	7·0
Inner Mongolia	7,338	782	10·7
Kansu and Ningsia	12,928	1,108	8·6
Shensi	15,881	1,572	9·9
Tibet	1,274	162	12·7
Total	582,603	77,257	13·3

Source: E. Ni, *Distribution of the Urban and Rural Population of Mainland China: 1953 and 1958*. US Bureau of the Census, International Population Reports, Series P-95, No. 56 (October 1960).

because Mao has a long-range view of history he is willing to accept temporary economic setbacks to assure long-range political purity, for, after all, 'politics and ideology are the motive power for everything'. Utilization and training of local labour, active local participation, stimulation of local innovation, lessening the technological gap between cities and countryside, all take priority over the Western-style model of technological and economic efficiency.

What then is the relationship of this policy of industrial diversification to future urban development? Is this an experiment likely to be reversed or will the industrialization of the countryside continue and eventually transform China's economy and society into a unique type at present unknown anywhere else in the world? It seems very likely that, discounting inevitable adjustments and fluctuations, the general trend of bringing industry to the people in the countryside, rather than shifting the peasants into the cities, will continue to be the long-range policy of China. It is also assumed that this will not result in the stagnation and deterioration of China's cities, since a considerable (and strategically most important) proportion of China's industry will continue to expand under central control and direction. In other words, rural industry developed primarily through local investment will supplement the large-scale urban economy but certainly will not replace it.

Quite probably China's cities will grow but at a relatively slow rate – much slower than might be expected in a reasonably healthy economy. The largest cities should increase at the slowest rate, while the most rapid growth should occur in towns under fifty thousand which in some ways would have closer ties to rural industrial development. Finally, the current understanding of what is 'urban' will no longer suffice and a new definition will have to be devised to accommodate the developments in the People's Republic. And in connection with this, in current writings one frequently encounters the statement that China is an overwhelmingly agricultural country, implying that she must therefore be a backward country. It is important to keep in mind that regardless of ideology or economic policy, China will continue to be 'an overwhelmingly agricultural country'. To use this fact as a significant gauge in measuring China's position on the developmental scale could result in major miscalculations.

4 · Population distribution and migration

Every reader of the world press has been exposed to descriptions of 'teeming China' – pictures of crowded cities and ant-like workers toiling over mass construction projects. What is so often forgotten is that population density varies strikingly in this country that covers an area of over 3·7 million square miles and that it is only 'teeming' in places. In fact, the admittedly high overall density of two hundred persons per square mile is only one-third the density of Britain and not nearly as high as it is in other countries of Asia and Europe.

Rational consideration of the problem in China must be taken from the viewpoint of spatial distribution of the population. In China, as in all nonindustrial countries, population settlement follows arable land, and her topography and climate so limit the area on which crops can be grown that only eleven or twelve per cent of the land is at present cultivated. As a result, some ninety-five per cent of the people live on only forty per cent of the land area. The most densely populated areas cover most of the lower Yangtze delta and the North China plain. In some of these central and coastal provinces densities of 1,000 persons per square mile are not uncommon, while in the Chengtu Plain in Szechwan Province it approaches an urban-like density of 2,500. But then vast areas of China, for the most part on her periphery, are virtually uninhabited: the four least densely populated provinces – Inner Mongolia, Sinkiang, Tsinghai and Tibet – contain just over half of the area of the country but less than four per cent of the population.

Table 8 presents the overall provincial population densities and the more meaningful densities based only on cultivated land. Although provinces with less fertile lands continue to have a lower population density, the number of drastic differences has been greatly reduced. These differences would be even further minimized if the calculation

Table 8: Population distribution and density in relation to total and cultivated land area

province	1957 population[1] (in thousands)	total area[2]		cultivated area[3]	
		sq. miles	density	sq. miles	density
NE					
Heilungkiang	14,860	178,996	83	28,000	531
Kirin	12,550	72,201	174	17,980	698
Liaoning	24,090	57,683	418	18,240	1,321
N					
Shansi	15,960	60,656	263	17,210	927
Hopei	48,730	84,316	578	33,910	1,437
Shantung	54,030	59,189	913	35,710	1,513
Honan	48,670	64,479	755	33,390	1,458
C					
Hupei	30,790	72,394	425	16,700	1,844
Hunan	36,220	81,274	446	14,900	2,431
Kiangsi	18,610	63,631	292	10,790	1,725
E					
Kiangsu	52,130	41,699	1,250	23,890	2,182
Anhwei	33,560	54,015	621	22,610	1,484
Chekiang	25,280	39,305	643	8,480	2,981
SE					
Fukien	14,650	47,529	308	5,650	2,592
Kwangtung	37,960	82,857	458	14,900	2,548
Kwangsi	19,390	91,583	212	9,760	1,986
SW					
Kweichow	16,890	67,181	251	7,960	2,121
Yunnan	19,100	168,417	113	10,530	1,814
Szechwan	72,160	219,150	329	29,800	2,421
NW					
Sinkiang	5,640	641,930	9	6,680	844
Tsinghai	2,050	278,378	7	1,540	1,331
Inner Mongolia	9,200	501,930	18	21,320	432
Kansu and Ningsia	14,610	135,298	96	21,060	694
Shensi	18,130	75,598	240	19,270	941
Tibet	1,270	472,200	3	n.a.	n.a.
Total	646,530	3,711,889	174	430,280	1,503

were to include only lands sown to food crops and if double- and triple-cropped lands were taken into consideration.

Considering the uneven density of Chinese population, why has population pressure not forced a more equitable spatial distribution of the people? Two simple and obvious reasons have already been mentioned: terrain and climate. Most of China is not hospitable to human habitation, being hilly and mountainous; about sixty per cent of the high area lies more than 6,000 feet above sea level and extensive areas in the west exceed 12,000 feet. Hundreds of thousands of square miles consist of generally flat to rolling desert plains. In the west these desert plains run into the equally dry Tarim and Dzungarian Basins which are separated by the lofty, largely barren ranges of the Tien Shan Mountains; extending eastward, the plains merge with the sandy and gravelly Gobi. The climate of China is highly diverse, ranging from tropical and subtropical in the south to subarctic in the extreme north-eastern provinces. Most of the country is arid; although some locations in the south-east have an average annual rainfall of above one hundred inches, large parts of northern and north-western China receive less than ten inches of rain a year. Thus, the settled areas of China are encircled by regions of nonproductive soils with insufficient rainfall, unsuitable topography, or both – areas of intense summer heat or of long winters with only relatively short growing seasons. Certainly only the most extreme pressures would make people move onto such lands.

In addition to topography and climate, the Chinese cultural and social structures have worked against extensive long-distance migration. Such factors as attachment to family and native village, the veneration of ancestors and regional language differences have influenced the natives against leaving their ancestral homes.

There was also the economic factor. For the majority of the Chinese

---

1 *Ten Great Years,* State Statistical Bureau (Peking: Foreign Language Press, 1960), p. 11.

2 *Ti-li Chih-shih* (Geographical Knowledge), No. 9 (1959), pp. 390–1, as converted into square miles in J. Aird, 'Population Growth and Distribution in Mainland China', *An Economic Profile of Mainland China,* Joint Economic Committee of the US Congress (Washington: February 1967), p. 370. It is unusual to find two sources that give identical areas for the provinces.

3 Data for 1957 as collected by D. H. Perkins, *Agricultural Development in China 1368–1968,* p. 236. Converted from millions of *shih mou* into square miles.

peasants, savings were virtually unknown; if a family had managed to improve its lot, a natural calamity or a man-made political upheaval very likely soon wiped out all the gains. Only an unusual attraction or a severe crisis could induce a family or an individual with little money to leave the home village with all its familiar attachments and venture out into the unknown, to break up and clear new lands of marginal agricultural value. Likewise, there was the problem of subsistence in an area where transportation was at best primitive but more often non-existent during the long wait for the first crop. A family that managed to accumulate some money stood a much better chance of success, especially since the turn of the century, by taking boat and heading for south-east Asia.

Despite all these inhibiting factors, in 3,000 years the Chinese people, slowly and perseveringly, spread from the middle reaches of the Yellow River to settle much of the Asian continent.

Early population movements

Large population movements were effected through gradual expansion rather than by long-distance migration. The shifting population first spread into the most arable valleys and, as their numbers increased, widened their search. Less fertile lands which took more effort to clear and ready for agriculture were also sites for new settlers. As farmers seeking an appropriate climate for their 'garden'-type agriculture, the Chinese throughout their early history tended to move southward, but as suitable land became more and more scarce they turned to the high plateaus and deserts to the west and the cool regions to the north, displacing or absorbing the weaker ethnic groups that were encountered. The distinct differences that exist between the northern and southern Chinese reflect the differences in the characteristics of the peoples with which they mixed during the centuries of expanding frontiers.

In cases where adjacent territories did not lend themselves to expansion, it was often famine and disease that reduced the growing population and re-established a reasonable balance between people and resources. In addition to the search for food, other stimuli leading to large shifts in the country's population included internal political chaos, border conflicts with nomadic tribes and severe droughts and floods which affected the peasants' ability to produce food for many subsequent years. The general nature of Chinese migration over the millennia can be summarized in the words of the historian C. P. Fitzgerald: 'The history of China is the record of an expanding culture, more than that of a conquering empire.'

During the more recent period, the province of Szechwan represents a good example of the westward spread of China's population. For almost two hundred years, between 1650 and 1850, this province – specifically the fertile Red Basin – was the primary recipient of migrants from the eastern provinces of China. Most of those who eventually reached Szechwan, however, had moved inland over several generations – each moving further west in search of new agricultural lands, so that the people from Kiangsi poured into Hupei and Hunan and those from Hupei and Hunan moved to Szechwan. Historical figures are admittedly inaccurate, but they can suggest the general volume of migration that must have taken place. The population of Szechwan increased from 8·6 million in 1787 to 44·2 million by 1850 and to 62·3 million by 1953. These figures are particularly impressive when it is remembered that during most of this period the annual natural increase of the population was well below one per cent.

In some instances population advanced and then receded like ocean waves, moving back into regions that had been vacated several scores or hundreds of years earlier. Thus provinces that were the source of migrants in one era due to the push of famine, drought, disease or war, were likely in another age to receive migrants after conditions improved and the land was once again agriculturally fit. By way of encouraging the people to return to depopulated regions, some rulers even offered land, tax exemptions and other incentives to the resettlers.

An example of this reverse migration followed the Taiping Rebellion, which lasted from 1850 to 1864 and resulted in major upheavals in China. Although the effects of the Taiping Wars were felt throughout the country, the most affected areas were the lower Yangtze provinces of Kiangsu, Chekiang, Anhwei and Kiangsi. Estimates vary, but at least twenty million persons were killed during these bloody wars. Some figures put it as high as fifty million, but this undoubtedly includes deaths caused by the famine and disease which accompanies the movements of a rabble military force. Whatever the number of losses, the Taipings made shambles of many towns and laid waste to extensive agricultural lands.

Conditions improved somewhat after 1864, and the depopulated provinces which then contained some of the country's best irrigated lands became particularly attractive to millions of peasants from Hupei, Hunan and other provinces – some of whose ancestors had moved out of these same lower-Yangtze lands decades or centuries before.

Major migration during the first half of the twentieth century was directed towards the north into the region commonly called Manchuria. Originally sparsely populated by peoples whose racial affinities were more with the Mongols, this area in ancient times had few Chinese settlers, all concentrated in the southern part of the Liaotung Peninsula. The trickle of Chinese into the regions north of the Great Wall had persisted for hundreds of years, accelerating during some periods and slackening when official restrictions on free migration came in. Following the spurt of migration during the latter part of the nineteenth century, the estimated population of this northern region at the turn of the century was fourteen million, of which eighty per cent were Chinese.

Manchuria represents perhaps the best recent example in which the 'pull' of opportunity was at least as great as the 'push' of adversity in initiating the northward flow of people. The rapid economic development of southern Manchuria after the 1905 occupation by the Japanese attracted hundreds of thousands of Chinese agricultural labourers. Although some of them settled there permanently, more than half of the young males who migrated from the adjacent provinces of Hopei, Shansi and Shantung during these years went home to their native villages after the harvest, often to return again the following year.

The continued civil wars and famines in north China and the inducement of cut-rate fares offered by both Chinese and Japanese rail and steamship companies increased the volume of migration into Manchuria in the 1920s. This mass movement, reaching a peak of over 800,000 in the year 1927, consisted of many more families than in the past and was much more permanent in nature. From 1923 to the end of 1930 almost 3·3 million migrants settled in Manchuria. The farmers from north China penetrated inland along the rapidly expanding railway system, settling on the land and providing cheap labour for Manchuria's expanding urban economy. Despite Japanese restrictions on migration in the 1930s, by 1940 the total population of the region (somewhat larger at that time than the present three provinces of north-east China) was enumerated by the Japanese at 44·5 million. All in all, during the first half of this century, perhaps as many as thirty million Chinese moved from famine-stricken areas of the Yellow River basin to the empty northern spaces of Manchuria – one of the major migrations in world history.

Migration since 1949

Ever since the initial exodus of some two million Chinese to the island of Taiwan and several hundred thousand to Hong Kong after 1949, China has had, for all practical purposes, a closed population. Article 11 of the regulations of the People's Republic covering the punishment of counterrevolutionaries states that 'those who secretly cross the border of the country for counterrevolutionary purposes will be punished with five or more years of imprisonment, life imprisonment or death'. Since in Peking's view almost anyone who wishes to leave the country is by definition a counterrevolutionary, very few have managed to leave. Exceptions are some 13,000 refugees who left Tibet for India in 1959 and 1960; the 50,000 or so Kazakhs who crossed the border from Sinkiang into the Soviet Union in the spring of 1962; the almost 100,000 refugees who entered Hong Kong during the same time period; and the estimated average of 10,000 Chinese who each year manage to avoid detection and slip across the border into Hong Kong.

At the same time there was a compensating movement of those who returned to China from other Asian countries. It is difficult to find any reliable figures on these repatriates, but it is well known that their number fluctuated with changing conditions in and out of the country. By promising special favours, Peking managed to persuade hundreds of thousands of overseas Chinese to return during the 1950s – many of them students who came back to study in special schools established for overseas Chinese. Probably the largest single migration followed the anti-Chinese riots in Indonesia. Some 90,000 refugees returned to China from Indonesia in 1960, and almost 5,000 following the more severe repressions in 1966. All in all, several million Chinese have been repatriated during the past twenty years. Whereas in and of themselves the figures seem fairly large, they are insignificant in terms of China's total population and of greater political than demographic interest.

As for the volume of internal migration, with the exception of a handful of national figures reported in the 1950s, meaningful statistics on long-range population movements are rare indeed. More common

figures referring to a city or an administrative unit are often not tied
down to a specific time period; conversely, some reports give a precise
time-frame but refer only to 'large numbers' of migrants. It is most
aggravating to find a precise figure of the number of people who turned
out at the railway station to bid farewell to those leaving for distant
provinces with no hint of the number of persons actually departing.

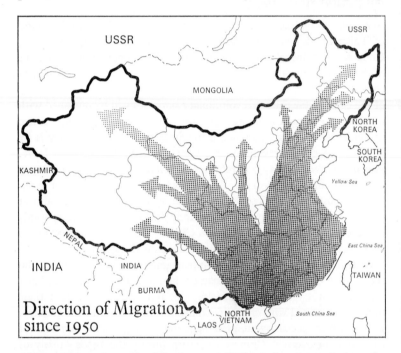

Direction of Migration since 1950

Although the place of origin is more likely to be reported than the
destination of the migrants, references to long-range migrants imply
most frequently a movement into the border provinces of Sinkiang,
Tsinghai, Kansu, Ningsia, Inner Mongolia or Heilungkiang.

Although it is quite obvious that statistical estimates must be extremely tenuous, there are a number of possible generalizations which
seem to hold for most of the first twenty years of the Communist regime:
(1) Clearly the movement continued towards the northern and western
provinces. (2) The number of people migrating fluctuated over the
years, depending on how vigorously Peking tried to influence migration
during a particular period. (3) Despite the bravado of the 'volunteers',

there are few who migrated of their own free will, without first under-going intensive ideological prodding. (4) It would appear that a dis-proportionate number of migrants came from the cities, although in many instances they were recent in-migrants from the surrounding rural areas. (5) Whatever may have been the actual number of long-range migrants, their departure made no demographic dent in the areas they left; their number is economically and politically significant, how-ever, for the sparsely settled regions that they went to.

Ignoring the natural barriers which have in fact caused the uneven distribution of China's population, Peking instead pointed to the foreign interests which had stimulated the tremendous growth of port cities and blamed the capitalistic exploitation and political and economic control by imperialists and other reactionary classes prior to 1949 for the problem. Although not specifically intended to correct this condition, during the 1950s there were two basic policies and goals that caused people to move from the densely populated coastal provinces. First, there was the effort to increase the country's cultivated land area; and second, there was the policy to increase the industrial production capacity of the interior provinces.

As with almost all statistics pertaining to the People's Republic, there is considerable disagreement as to the amount of potentially productive agricultural land in China. According to some specialists, because of existing population pressures which force the peasants to cultivate remote valleys and terrace steep hills and mountains, prac-tically all the land suitable for growing crops is currently being utilized. On the other hand, the most optimistic Chinese estimates are that the extent of agricultural land available in the mid 1950s could be doubled. The truth, as is usually the case, lies somewhere between these two extremes. If the cost-factor is disregarded, it is possible that China's arable areas could perhaps be increased by twenty-five to thirty per cent, from about 270 million acres in the middle 1950s to about 350 million at some distant date.

What is theoretically possible with regard to expanding arable land is entirely unrealistic in terms of what China is now capable of doing. Clearly any large and lasting land reclamation project can only be pursued with the use of heavy machinery and large engineering endeavours – that is, with heavy capital investment. Having neither the necessary equipment nor the capital, the Chinese have been attempting to increase agricultural lands primarily through the investment of

F

abundant labour power. The First Five-Year Plan (1953–7) called for the total reclamation of some sixteen million acres of wasteland. Success was achieved mainly in increasing arable areas in regions that were already agriculturally productive by expanding irrigation works, by building additional terraces up hillsides and by other activities which could extend existing cultivation through the efforts of thousands of people armed with picks and shovels. But when it came to opening up wastelands in China's remote provinces, such methods were not very effective: it is safe to assume not only that the goal set for the Five-Year Plan was not met, but that in many cases land retrieved for agriculture through simple earth-work reverted to wasteland within just a few years.

In the context of the current discussion, however, the principal question is how many people were moved into distant provinces to engage in land reclamation and agriculture. During the first years of the Communist regime there was no large-scale, planned migration programme; until 1955 only about 600,000 persons were reported to have been relocated – most of them within their respective or adjacent provinces. In 1956 the regime initiated what was to become the most massive migration of the decade. It was reported that during that single year 725,000 persons were moved, of whom 292,000 (forty per cent) were resettled within their provinces and 433,000 (sixty per cent) were transferred into the more distant western and northern provinces. All of them were moved in conjunction with 'planned resettlement for reclamation of wasteland'. This rapid movement of hordes of people brought about inevitable confusion, forcing even the Ministry of Interior to admit 'there were certain defects in the work connected with resettlement'. Backtracking was in order, and the number of migrants declined almost as rapidly as it had increased. The next year, 1957, was designated as a year for consolidating the resettlement programme, but the planned 1958 long-distance migration of 300,000 was probably nothing more than an inflated Great Leap figure. Thus, no matter what assumptions are made with regard to the above figures, the total number of long-range migrants who left central China to open and work new lands could not have exceeded two million and is much more likely to be closer to one million.

The other policy in operation during this time-frame and affecting migration was related to the construction and expansion of China's industrial capabilities in the interior of the country. The growth of the interior was not immediate. In 1952–3, when existing industries were being rebuilt, over two-thirds of the total industrial growth occurred in the coastal provinces which traditionally were the scene for the overwhelming proportion of gross industrial production. The First Five-Year Plan, however, stressed industrial development in new regions, and during the 1953–5 period fifty-five per cent of all capital investment was directed towards the interior, establishing a pattern which persisted through most of that decade.

In terms of population, this phase of development naturally resulted in the growth of inland cities. Data are not available to show the differential rates of urbanization in the various provinces, but there are figures to show the fantastic growth of individual cities in the provinces of the west and north. For example, between 1953 and 1959, Urumchi (Sinkiang) increased from 140,700 to 700,000; Pao-t'ou (Inner Mongolia), from 149,000 to 800,000; Lan-chou (Kansu), from 397,400 to 1,000,000; Hsi-ning (Tsinghai), from 93,000 to 400,000; and many smaller towns increased at an even faster rate.

Nevertheless, interregional migration contributed little to this urban growth, for most of it was the result of the resettlement of peasants from within the province. As long as unskilled labour – so vital for China's construction projects – was available locally, it was unnecessary to use the limited transportation facilities for this type of worker. But a variety of specialists was also required by the expanding industrial bases, such as petroleum engineers for Sinkiang, skilled steel workers for the new steel centre in Pao-t'ou, and engineers, medical personnel, teachers, bookkeepers and managers for all the growing cities. Most of these came from large cities such as Shanghai and Tientsin, and from the highly industrialized province of Liaoning. Because these technical personnel could not have been conveniently spared by the existing plants and factories, their number could not have been too large and the total number of migrants associated with long-distance urban-migration certainly did not exceed one million.

What other national policies prevailed which resulted in long-range migration during the decade of the fifties? The Communists deliberately tried to settle Han Chinese in the areas populated by minority nationalities, allegedly to educate these groups and modernize their economy, but more often to consolidate control over them (see chapter 5). Since most of the agricultural and industrial development was already taking place in the minority regions, both purposes were served by the new migrants, although individuals sent specifically to assist and control the minorities were relatively few in number. References to veterans moving into the border provinces are undoubtedly valid, but to consider them independently would result once again in double-counting, since they constitute just another segment of the population that was involved in the migration figures already considered. Road- and rail-building programmes and other large construction projects in the western and northern provinces utilized hundreds of thousands of labourers, but only a small proportion of them would normally have crossed provincial boundaries. They were usually recruited from the general area of the project and returned to their homes when the project was completed – a practice that is still in effect.

Flimsy though the figures for the 1950s are, the data became even more unsatisfactory for the decade of the 1960s so that only a very general discussion of the trends in long-distance migration is possible.

Following the failure of the industrially-oriented Great Leap Forward, the party reversed its priorities, declared agriculture the foundation of the national economy and called on all people to 'concentrate forces on strengthening the agricultural front'. This intensified China's almost perpetual *hsia fang* or 'down to the countryside' movement (discussed in more detail in chapter 3). Although from 1960 to 1966 as many as two million persons reportedly participated in the 'down to the country-side' movement, only relatively few in number were involved in long-distance migration, since most followed Peking's directive to return to their places of origin – usually rural areas within the province or the province adjacent to it. Only occasionally did the press mention groups going to 'the frontier' or the 'border areas' or to specific border provinces.

Furthermore, the two policies most responsible for the long-distance migration during the 1950s – to increase cultivated land area and industrial production – were not being implemented to the same extent in the early 1960s. The rural areas of the western and northern provinces were still attempting to assimilate the migrants who had arrived in the previous years, while neither the national nor the provincial budgets could allocate any sizeable sums of money for land reclamation during this period of economic difficulties. Industrial development in the border provinces suffered as it did in the country as a whole, so that western and northern cities were just as concerned about moving out post-Leap excess manpower as were the cities in other parts of China.

Thus, long-distance migration in association with either agriculture or industrial growth probably did not resume to any significant proportion until 1964.

In the summer of 1966 another disruption to life in China was caused by the Cultural Revolution. The Red Guard movement which encouraged young people to travel around the country and to participate in 'long marches' in order to 'exchange revolutionary experiences' set literally millions of people in motion. Once again, however, this did not result in any permanent mass migration into the border provinces. On the contrary, 'misinformed revolutionary youths' were accused of deserting their production posts in the rural areas of the interior and creating an 'evil blast of returning to the cities'. A typical example was reported in the February 1967 issue of *Wen Hui Pao* which stated that 'Numerous young builders of Sinkiang have returned to Shanghai, thus seriously affecting spring sowing in that province'. On balance, then, there were probably more people who left the border provinces than moved into them during the first two years of the Cultural Revolution.

By the spring of 1968 the regime finally reached the conclusion that it was necessary to halt Red Guard travel, get the youths back to school and reduce the general confusion in the country. Although the problem of smothering the seething Cultural Revolution was not an easy one, the first step was to move the Red Guards back to the areas from which they had come. This effort gradually went over into the broader policy, growing out of changes in the philosophy of education, of transferring large numbers of school-age youth out of the cities. Eventually, this new *hsia fang* movement was extended to include even broader segments of the urban population. Repeating over and over Mao's prescription that 'it is necessary for educated young people to go to the countryside and be re-educated by the poor and lower-middle class peasants', the literal and figurative process of rounding up mainly young people for 'deportation' to the countryside prevailed throughout China for several years. Particular attention was also directed at the parents, warning them not to allow harmful notions of 'love for one's children to interfere with Chairman Mao's plans' nor to try to keep their children 'in the greenhouse and turn them into sprouts of revisionism'. Despite intensive persuasion, the youth were not too enthusiastic about the prospect of leaving the cities and being separated from their family. Opposition, of course, was never openly admitted by the press, but the

Table 9 : Estimated provincial population distribution : 1970
(population in thousands)

province	(1) population 1953	(2) population 1957	(3) average annual growth rate 1953–7 (in per cent)
NE			
Heilungkiang	11,897	14,860	5·54
Kirin	11,290	12,550	2·48
Liaoning	20,566	24,090	3·81
N			
Shansi	14,314	15,960	2·56
Hopei	43,348	48,730	2·76
Shantung	48,877	54,030	2·34
Honan	44,215	48,670	2·24
C			
Hupei	27,790	30,790	2·40
Hunan	33,227	36,220	2·00
Kiangsi	16,773	18,610	2·43
E			
Kiangsu	47,137	52,130	2·45
Anhwei	30,663	33,560	2·10
Chekiang	22,866	25,280	2·35
SE			
Fukien	13,143	14,650	2·55
Kwangtung	36,740	37,960	0·74
Kwangsi	17,591	19,390	2·27
SW			
Kweichow	15,037	16,890	2·74
Yunnan	17,473	19,100	2·07
Szechwan	65,685	72,160	2·19
NW			
Sinkiang	4,874	5,640	3·49
Tsinghai	1,676	2,050	4·96
Inner Mongolia	7,338	9,200	5·64
Kansu and Ningsia	12,928	14,610	2·89
Shensi	15,881	18,130	3·15
Tibet	1,274	1,270	—
Total	582,603	646,530	

(4) projection to 1970 using 1953-7 growth rate	(5) adjusted to 1970 estimated total population	(6) reported populations (unspecified date)	(7) 1970 final distribution
22,753	20,964	21,000	20,700
15,910	14,659	17,000	17,500
33,496	30,863	28,000	30,500
20,360	18,756	18,000	18,600
63,089	58,130	54,000	57,500
67,748	62,422	57,000	61,800
60,056	55,335	50,000	54,800
38,795	35,745	32,000	35,400
44,192	40,718	38,000	40,300
23,499	21,652	22,000	21,400
65,417	60,275	57,000	59,600
41,288	38,042	35,000	37,600
31,733	29,238	31,000	28,900
18,674	17,206	17,000	17,000
41,226	37,985	40,000	41,000
24,181	22,280	24,000	22,000
21,835	20,119	17,000	19,900
23,442	21,599	23,000	21,400
89,424	82,394	70,000	81,500
7,681	7,077	8,000	8,500
3,048	2,808	2,000	2,800
14,167	13,053	13,000	12,900
19,093	17,592	15,000	17,400
24,136	22,239	21,000	22,000
2,000	1,844	1,320	2,000
817,243	753,000	711,320	753,000

For Note see next page.

articles and letters to the editors discussing Mao's dictum left no doubt about the general feelings of the youth being moved.

The volume of this latest movement is once again impossible to quantify, although it certainly ran into the millions with some estimates running into tens of millions. As in previous movements of this type, the substance of the numerous reports would lead to the deduction that a relatively small proportion of the transferred population was sent over long distances into border provinces which would find it economically difficult to absorb large numbers of people.

Current levels of migration

After the above generalizations with regard to population movements in China during the past twenty years, is there a way to get at the present provincial distribution of the population and obtain some

---

Column 1: 30 June 1953 census figures in 1957 boundaries from *Chung-hua jen-min kung-ho-guo ti-t'u-chi* (Atlas of the People's Republic of China) (Peking: 1957).

Column 2: Ten Great Years, State Statistical Bureau (Peking: 1960), p. 11. Figures are for the end of 1957.

Column 3: Average annual growth rate for the period of June 1953 to end of 1957 (4½ years).

Column 4: Projection of the 1953 base populations to 1 January 1970 on the assumption that the differential growth rates of individual provinces (column 3) continued. The population of Tibet was arbitrarily set at two million.

Column 5: Population of the provinces adjusted downward proportionately to add up to my independently estimated 1970 population of 753·0 million (see table 3).

Column 6: Provincial populations reported by the Revolutionary Committees and released by the New China News Agency in scattered reports in 1968 and 1969, and possibly referring to the 1965–6 time period. Because the origin of these figures continues to be a mystery, they are used only as a general guide.

Column 7: A comparison of the projected and adjusted figures in column 5 with the reported 'mid-1960s' figures in column 6 shows a reasonable congruence for most of the provinces. In only four are the projected figures deemed unreasonable and therefore adjusted on the basis of the reported figures in column 6. Neither boundary changes nor migration can adequately explain an average annual rate of growth between 1953 and 1957 of less than one per cent for Kwangtung – generally agreed as an unusable figure. The other three provinces where adjustments were made are Kirin and Sinkiang, where the post-1957 migration must have been higher than the average during the previous four years, and Tibet, where the 1970 population was arbitrarily set at two million. Once the independent estimates for these four provinces were inserted, the other provincial figures were adjusted proportionately to add up to the estimated 1970 population of the country. The individual figures were then rounded to the nearest 100,000.

appreciation of the volume of migration into the provinces that are known to have accommodated most of the long-distance migrants? The following estimates are made with full realization of the pitfalls inherent in such calculations.

Table 9 presents the estimated 1970 distribution of the population by provinces. The calculation assumes that the 1953 and 1957 figures are the best available to us and that this time period was relatively typical so far as the direction and the relative volume of migration are concerned. Thus, each province is projected using its own annual growth rate to 1970. The resulting total population is then adjusted proportionately to the independently estimated total population (see chapter 2).

Since virtually all the migrants are Han (Chinese), one method to derive their number is through the ethnic composition of the border provinces. In table 10a the non-Han population for each border province is projected to 1970 and then subtracted from the estimated total 1970 population of the province. The difference represents the number of Han in the province in 1970. In table 10b the Han population already in the provinces as of 1953 is projected to 1970 and then subtracted from the estimated number of Han there in that year. The difference is considered to be the implied number of Han migrants during the preceding $16\frac{1}{2}$ years (June 1953 to January 1970). This method produces the following number of in-migrants:

province	migrants (1953–70)
Sinkiang	2,262,000
Kansu-Ningsia	689,000
Heilungkiang	5,323,000
Inner Mongolia	3,335,000
Tsinghai	633,000
Total	12,242,000

It must be stressed that the twelve-million figure represents nothing more than an order of magnitude. It is a figure, however, that seems reasonable and consistent with both the economic potential of the provinces of in-migration and the political forces that resulted in long-range migration.

Given the lack of data it is no more difficult to predict the future than to surmise the past. Although the natural 'pulls' and 'pushes' which set

Table 10a: Estimated number of Han (Chinese) in the border provinces: January 1970 (population in thousands)

province	nationality	30 June 1953		1 January 1970	
		population	% of total	population	% of total
Sinkiang	Uighur	3,640	74·7	4,707	55·4
	Kazakh	475	9·7	564	6·6
	Han	300	6·2	2,650	31·2
	Hui	200	4·1	259	3·0
	Mongol	120	2·5	155	1·8
	Kirghiz	70	1·4	91	1·1
	Other	69	1·4	74	·9
	Total	4,874	100·0	8,500	100·0
Inner	Han	6,309	85·2	11,489	89·1
Mongolia	Mongol	985	13·3	1,274	9·9
	Hui	52	·7	67	·5
	Manchu	21	·3	27	·2
	Other	33	·5	43	·3
	Total	7,400	100·0	12,900	100·0
Heilungkiang	Han	10,937	91·9	19,459	94·0
	Minorities	960	8·1	1,241	6·0
	Total	11,897	100·0	20,700	100·0
Kansu-	Han	11,428	88·4	15,460	88·9
Ningsia	Minorities	1,500	11·6	1,940	11·1
	Total	12,928	100·0	17,400	100·0
Tsinghai	Han	951	56·7	1,862	66·5
	Minorities	725	43·3	938	33·5
	Total	1,676	100·0	2,800	100·0

Methodological Note: The minority population of each province was projected from 30 June 1953 to 1 January 1970 using the national rate of population growth. Only two adjustments were made – both in Sinkiang: (1) an allowance was made for the estimated 50,000 Kazakhs who fled to the Soviet Union in 1962; and (2) it was assumed that most of the Russians (13,000 in 1953) left the province.

The projected minorities were then subtracted from the estimated provincial population for 1 January 1970 (see table 9). The figure thus derived for each of the provinces represents the estimated number of Han in that province.

The assumptions in this calculation are as follows:

1. The total population for China and its distribution is realistic and usable

Note continued on next page

Table 10b: Estimated number of Han (Chinese) migrants into the border provinces

| province | 1953[1] | Han population (in thousands) | | |
		1970 (projected)[2]	1970 (estimated)[3]	implied migrants[4]
Sinkiang	300	388	2,650	2,262
Inner Mongolia	6,309	8,154	11,489	3,335
Heilungkiang	10,937	14,136	19,459	5,323
Kansu-Ningsia	11,428	14,771	15,460	689
Tsinghai	951	1,229	1,862	633
Total	29,925	38,678	50,920	12,242

[1] See table 10a.
[2] 1953 figures projected to 1970 using the national rate of growth and assuming no migration.
[3] See table 10a.
[4] Difference between estimated and projected figures.

Obviously a very basic premise, but one that could make a significant difference, is the estimated number of migrants.

2. All the migrants were Han. This is a safe assumption since only a scant number of migrants from central China could belong to minority groups.

3. The natural increase of minority populations was identical with that of the total population of the People's Republic. Most likely both the birth and death rates among minorities were higher than those for the Han; however, there should not be any great divergencies in the natural increase (births minus deaths) among these populations. A minor adjustment in the natural increase would not basically change the results.

4. The progeny of the migrants are excluded from the calculation. By far the greatest number of Han migrants were unmarried youth – most of them males. Although many eventually married and raised a family in their new location, many others remained single either because of a shortage of females or because of prevailing living conditions. At any rate, the number of children born to migrants during an average of some ten years should not significantly affect the calculated number of migrants.

Source Note: The provincial figures of minorities for 1953 were obtained as follows: Sinkiang – M. Freeberne, 'Demographic and Economic Changes in the Sinkiang Uighur Autonomous Region', *Population Studies*, Vol. XX, No. 1 (July 1966), p. 108.

Inner Mongolia – *Nei-meng-ku tzu-chih-ch'u chung-chi-ho wen-hua chien-she ch'eng-chiu-ti t'ung-chi* (Statistical Achievements of the Inner Mongolian Autonomous Region) (Peking; 1960), translated by JPRS, No. 16,952 (3 January 1963).

Heilungkiang – On 5 April 1957 the New China News Agency (NCNA) reported: 'There are 411 primary and secondary schools and teacher training schools for the 960,000 people of minority nationalities in Heilungkiang Province.' Usually population figures cited in the mid 1950s referred to 1953. If, however, this is 1956 data, then the 1970 estimate of minorities is over-estimated and the number of Chinese is under-estimated by some 30,000.

Note continued overleaf.

people in motion are carefully controlled by Peking, many of the same economic, social, geographic, demographic and political factors are undoubtedly reflected in the prescribed population movements. 'Only' the personal considerations are missing – the search for individual opportunities. Thus, a moderate flow of population to the north and west should persist and the volume of this migratory movement will continue to depend on the availability of resources for the development of frontier provinces and on the vagaries of the Peking regime. It is certain, however, that the spatial distribution of the population of China will not change drastically despite any likely future ebb and flow of migrants.

Kansu-Ningsia – 'Areas where regional autonomy has been established embrace a total population of more than two million, of which more than 1·2 million are minority nationalities, accounting for over eighty per cent of the minority population in the province.' NCNA (15 June 1957). Once again the data are presumed to refer to 1953, and imply a total minority population of 1·5 million.

Tsinghai – 'Prior to liberation the province's population was only 1·4 million, of whom minority nationalities comprised half.' (*Min-tsu t'uan-chieh* [Nationalities Solidarity], JPRS 740-D, No. 2 (February 1959).) Assuming a minimal natural increase for the 700,000 minorities between 'pre-liberation' and the middle of 1953, a somewhat arbitrary figure of 725,000 is selected for the latter date.

5 · National minorities

National minorities, who in China now number over forty million, inevitably pose a dilemma for a communist government. The root cause may be traced back to Marx, who underestimated and misunderstood the forces of nationalism. Contending that all national distinctions would necessarily vanish through socialist victory, he nevertheless insisted on the right of self-determination. Lenin subsequently interpreted self-determination to include the right of political secession, but probably only because he considered this an unlikely possibility. He firmly believed that the abolition of oppression and prejudice in conjunction with practical economic considerations would cancel any desire on the part of lesser national groups to establish independent small states. Both Marx and Lenin looked forward to the 'inevitable' assimilation of all people and, in turn, to the elimination of all national differences.

Living with a dilemma

The contradictions between communist philosophies and the realities of the forces of nationalism have been haunting the People's Republic of China as they have the Soviet Union. Unfortunately for Peking, pretentious policies and announcements have elicited little enthusiasm from most of the minorities; nor have good will and sincerity been forthcoming from those expected to implement the policies. China has discovered that, not unlike giving a child sweets but forbidding him to eat them, you cannot stimulate the self-identity of minority groups while at the same time insisting this increased or even newly discovered self-identity be sublimated for some vague and alien cause.

As early as 1931 the First All-China Congress of the Soviets stipu-
lated that: 'The Chinese Soviet Government recognizes the right of
self-determination of the national minorities in China to the extent that
these minorities may detach themselves from China and form independent nations . . . or set up their own autonomous regions.' The
reference to secession could be tolerated only by a political party not in
power. Quite predictably, upon assuming control in 1949, the victorious
Communists immediately shifted the emphasis from 'secession' to
'autonomy' and the 1954 State Constitution stated unequivocally that
'national autonomous areas are the inalienable parts of the People's
Republic of China'.

The Inner Mongolian Autonomous Region was established on 1 May
1947, even before the Communists seized full control of China. The
Sinkiang Uighur Autonomous Region was established on 1 October
1955, Kwangsi Chuang Autonomous Region on 15 March 1958, and
Ningsia Hui Autonomous Region was formally inaugurated on 25
October 1958. Although the Preparatory Committee for Tibet was
inaugurated in 1956, political instability in the area prevented formaliza-
tion of the autonomous region until 9 September 1965. In addition to
the autonomous regions, by January 1955 the Communists had established twenty-six autonomous *ch'u* (districts) and twenty-six autonomous *hsien* (counties). Since then other units have been created and
many new boundaries have been drawn in order to accommodate
scattered minority populations: the number of autonomous districts
increasing to twenty-nine and autonomous counties to sixty-two by
January 1965. However, either because of political considerations and
intentional gerrymandering to assure a significant proportion of
Chinese in each autonomous area or because of the scattered distribution of many minority groups, in only a few instances do ethnic
groups constitute a majority of the established autonomous areas.

Although the creation of autonomous areas in no sense could be
translated into true 'self-determination', it must be admitted that for
almost ten years in the process of establishing controls, the Communists
made an effort to improve the inferior position of the minorities and, at
least at the national level, to cater to some of their needs.

The central government pledged itself to assist the minorities in every
phase of political, economic and agricultural advancement, launching
'socialist reformation and democratic reform at a rate that was appropriate to the local conditions'. Hundreds of articles and thousands of

dispatches described how the minorities prospered economically, conquered disease, and established widespread educational facilities. Furthermore, reflecting the policy that 'all the nationalities have freedom to use and foster the growth of their spoken and written languages', various language research and training activities were instituted by the Chinese Academy of Sciences through the Language Research Institute and the Central Institute of Nationalities in Peking and in the local branches. As written languages were being created for groups that never had one, historical and anthropological research was initiated in an attempt to acquaint the people with their past culture and, when possible, past glory.

It was only a matter of a few years, however, before the rosy picture in Chinese publications became tinged with caveats. Although slick illustrated magazines devoted to minority affairs continued to show, in colour, the love and cooperation existing between the Chinese and their minority brothers and to herald economic achievements and cultural discoveries, other communications media began diluting these reports with more and more 'buts' and 'howevers'. The basic problem was not difficult to detect: it was the combination of the inevitable friction between leaders and followers, and the traditional clashes between the Chinese and the minorities – all rolled into one.

It has already been mentioned that most autonomous areas did not contain a predominance of minorities even when they were originally created. Over the years, because of the influx of Han (discussed in the previous chapter), the proportion of national minorities steadily declined. Initially the in-migration of Chinese was relatively small, but in a sense more penetrating and disruptive in terms of the community and local society. They were cadres sent in by Peking to assist the local population. Most minorities lacked education and trained personnel not only to assume leadership positions but to perform even simple clerical and bookkeeping functions. This fact provided Peking with the excuse, if an excuse was in fact necessary, to send political, cultural and technical personnel of Han ancestry to train the minorities, to establish autonomous governments, and in some cases to study the mores and languages of these people. Thus, from the outset, the Han have pre-dominated in all party and government organizations and have controlled all the key positions, while the native contribution was relegated to the less significant stations.

Another form of Han in-migration followed the influx of Chinese

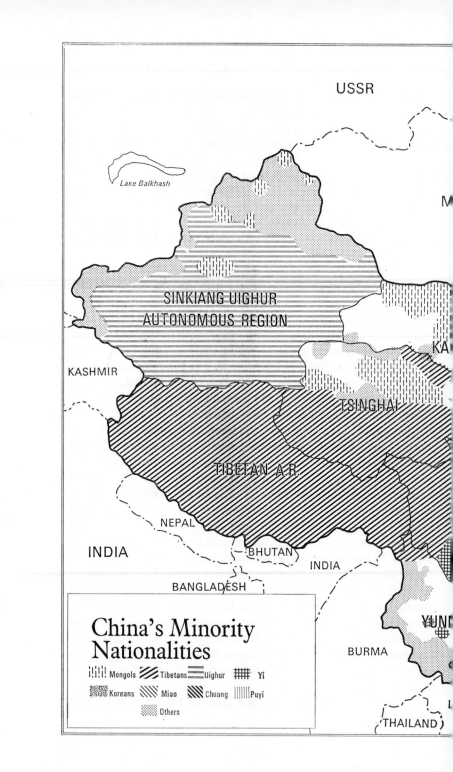

USSR

Lake Balkhash

M

SINKIANG-UIGHUR
AUTONOMOUS REGION

KA

KASHMIR

TSINGHAI

TIBETAN A.R.

NEPAL

INDIA

BHUTAN

INDIA

BANGLADESH

YUN

China's Minority Nationalities

BURMA

Mongols Tibetans Uighur Yi

Koreans Miao Chuang Puyi

Others

THAILAND

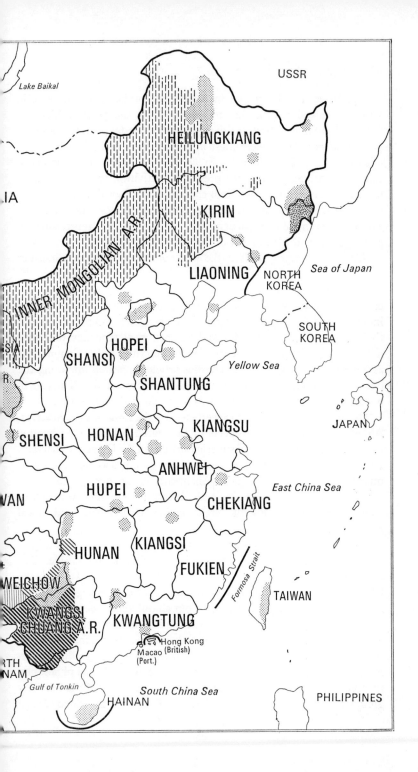

cadres. It was usually greater in volume but probably less abrasive in terms of relations with the minorities. Over the years millions of Chinese have moved from the densely-settled coastal provinces into the peripheral provinces where most minorities were located. Whether to open new lands for agriculture, to work in some of the growing urban centres or to engage in other prescribed activities, these migrants in most instances did not come into contact with minorities as directly as did the cadres. The increased proportion of Chinese, however, did assure an even greater participation of Han in the 'representative' governments and institutions of the autonomous administrative units.

Had the Chinese practised the philosophy towards the minorities that was enunciated in Peking's policy statements, friction between the two groups might not have developed. Unfortunately this was not the case. Most of the people who came were neither properly trained nor indoctrinated for the job, bringing with them the traditional sense of their own cultural superiority and the historical tendency to regard non-Han minority groups as 'barbarians' – described by the Communists as 'Great Han chauvinism'. Numerous articles appeared imploring the cadres to abandon the usual master-race concept of the Han and to fight indifference and apathy towards the needs of the minorities.

The situation was further exacerbated by the minorities themselves. Although lured by the prospects of the stated policies, they became irritated by the dogmatic and superior attitude of the Chinese leadership. Despite these frustrations, however, many groups accepted the Communist 'carrot' and strove more vehemently for greater autonomy and self-determination. These demands in turn were met with bitter attacks and accusations of 'great nation chauvinism' and 'local nationalism'.

This intensity of feelings grew, and many of the programmes originally intended to provide minorities with cultural pride and self-identification gradually lapsed. The Great Leap Forward, which was to make China into an industrialized modern nation through 'maogic', was the last straw. In their eagerness to wipe out all differences between people and make everyone a worker, a peasant, a soldier and a student at one and the same time, the Communists abandoned their efforts to stress the differences of the minorities and their policy of gradualism in nationality affairs. But they did not publicly reinstate the old philosophy that sinification would enrich and develop the cultures of the minority groups and raise their standard of living. There was no stated change in the policies pursued before 1958 – policies which are still in the books and which are periodically revived, depending on the mood of the times. But custom and traditions unlike those of the Han were frowned on; the cadres insisted on rapid changes in 'decadent' minority practices; Chinese was reintroduced in most areas as the official language and as the primary tongue at all educational levels; and sinification of the minorities was for all practical purposes resumed. In 1958 Prime Minister Chou En-lai explained that in view of its superior numbers the Han race had to play the leading role.

The resulting dissatisfaction with Peking's coercive policies erupted into a number of scattered local revolts, news of which leaked out to the outside world. No doubt many more unreported uprisings were initiated by the restive minorities during the communization of China. The most publicized revolt occurred of course in Tibet where anti-Chinese feelings, intensifying over the years, terminated in wide-spread opposition in 1958, armed revolt and the flight of the Dalai Lama in 1959.

In the 1960s dispatches dealing with minority problems fell off drastically and finally the only scholarly journal devoted to minorities (*Nationalities Research*) ceased publication. Nevertheless, the more pragmatic policies restored by Peking following the economic crisis of the early 1960s must have relieved some of the pressures in the minority areas as well. The active sinification process was probably interrupted, but the earlier effort to increase the self-identity of the minorities was not reintroduced. It needed a Great Proletarian Cultural Revolution to disturb once again the very precarious status quo of the minorities: nationalism, it prophesied, at the expense of patriotism creates schism among the people. Even though radio dispatches from Peking and from the capitals of the various autonomous regions applauded China's minorities for participating actively in attacking 'revisionism' and the 'towering crimes' of Liu Shao-ch'i and his henchmen, there is every reason to believe that the serious clashes between the various blocks of Mao-supporters were intensified by the division, in many cases, of the Red Guards into the Chinese and minority factions. After all, the Cultural Revolution was designed to eradicate the 'four olds' (religious beliefs, traditional culture, customs and habits) which were especially strongly entrenched among the minority nationalities.

The developments described above, already brief and general, require little summation. It is obvious that China's national policies, even those specifically directed at the minorities, have not affected all groups in the same way. Various policies and campaigns had an effect on the nomadic peoples different than on those minorities involved primarily in agriculture, and different again than on those who were urban based. And although it is conceivable that the more backward peoples in the mountains of Yunnan lived through the Great Leap and the Cultural Revolution in complete ignorance of these upheavals, they would be the exception to the rule. It would seem safe to predict that China will strive to broaden her controls over the minorities both by increasing political pressures and by gradually settling more and more Han in the areas currently inhabited by minorities.

And yet, while the strategic importance of some of the minority areas – Sinkiang for example with its atomic test site at Lop Nor – almost certainly precludes true autonomy, the Chinese nevertheless must consider developments on the Soviet side of the border. Here, Moscow is making every effort to emphasize the well-being of the Moslem population in the USSR. Central Asia, especially the Ferghana Valley, is made into a showcase for the benefit of Moslems in the Third World and, specifically, for those in China. Presumably, despite verbal invectives and clashes between the two countries, the Moslem minorities in the Soviet Union and in China remain in contact, so that the Uighurs for example are well aware that the Uzbek, Tadzhik and Kirghiz minority groups across the border enjoy living standards that are much higher than theirs. The Chinese Communists must be extremely careful that the pressures from Peking and the real or imagined enticements from Moscow do not combine to produce a major crisis on the border.

Numbers and distribution

The 1953 census-registration reported a total of 35,320,0c0 persons belonging to minority nationalities, consisting of some fifty non-Han groups, and constituting approximately six per cent of China's total population. Many questions come to mind in connection with the national minority figures as reported by the Communists and presented in table 11.

The problems discussed earlier in connection with the accuracy of the 1953 population statistics (see chapter 1) are particularly relevant to the minorities. No doubt the overwhelming majority of the 8,397,477

Table 11 : National minorities in the People's Republic : 1953

nationality	number[1] (in thousands)	language group	provinces of primary location
Chuang	7,030	Chuang-Thai	Kwangsi, Yunnan, etc.
Uighur	3,640	Turkic	Sinkiang
Hui	3,559	Chinese	Ningsia, Kansu, etc.
Yi	3,254	Tibeto-Burmese	Szechwan, Yunnan, etc.
Tibetan	2,776	Tibeto-Burmese	Tibet, Szechwan, Tsinghai, etc.
Miao	2,511	Miao-Yao	Kweichow, Yunnan, Hunan, etc.
Manchu	2,419	Tungus-Manchurian	Liaoning, Kirin, Heilungkiang, etc
Mongol	1,463	Mongolian	Inner Mongolia, Liaoning, etc.
Puyi	1,248	Chuang-Thai	Kweichow
Korean	1,120	Korean	Kirin, etc.
Tung	713	Chuang-Thai	Kweichow, etc.
Yao	666	Miao-Yao	Kwangsi
Pai	567	Tibeto-Burmese	Yunnan
Tuchia	549	Tibeto-Burmese	Hunan, Hupei
Kazakh	509	Turkic-Burmese	Sinkiang
Hani	481	Tibeto-Burmese	Yunnan
Thai	479	Chuang-Thai	Yunnan
Li	361	Chuang-Thai	Kwangtung
Lisu	317	Tibeto-Burmese	Yunnan
Kawa	286	Mon-Khmer	Yunnan
She	219	Miao-Yao	Fukien, Chekiang
Tunghsiang	156	Mongolian	Kansu
Nasi	143	Tibeto-Burmese	Yunnan
Lahu	139	Tibeto-Burmese	Yunnan
Shui	134	Chuang-Thai	Kweichow
Chingpo	102	Tibeto-Burmese	Yunnan
Other	479		The majority in Yunnan, Sinkiang, Inner Mongolia, Tsinghai, Kansu
Total	35,320		

For Notes see next page.

persons who were 'surveyed indirectly' because they were located in 'remote areas where communications facilities were poor' were in the sparsely settled minority areas. At best, estimates were made by the Commission on Minority Affairs on the basis of samples and surveys; at worst, they were simply guesses. Certainly figures reported to the nearest individual imply a precision inconceivable under the conditions then prevailing.

In addition to the known statistical errors inherent in the data on minorities, it is also apparent that the Chinese were a little over-zealous in their efforts to identify and list the groups. What criteria were used to identify minorities? How extensive and how objective was the official prompting on nationality? It is quite probable, for example, that many individuals were confused as to their nationality and had to be 'helped' by the registrar. Assuming a choice was involved, were there any advantages to be derived from listing oneself as a Han rather than as a member of some minority? Some of the minority people, especially in the urban areas, could and probably did pass for Chinese. Also, it is known that in mixed marriages the parents of children below eighteen were allowed to select their offspring's nationalities; undoubtedly the nationality believed to be most advantageous was chosen. To what extent was the reporting influenced by political considerations? Although instructions were specific – no revision or alterations were allowed on local reports – what was the case when the final tabulations were made in Peking?

The 2,419,000 Manchus listed in the 1953 census, for example, can only be interpreted as political fiction. The Manchus, historically located in Manchuria and north China, have been virtually assimilated into the Han ethnic group: it is estimated that no more than a couple of

---

[1] S. I. Bruk, *Chislennost' i Rasseleniye Narodov Mira* (Numbers and Distribution of the Peoples of the World) (Moscow: 1962), pp. 17, 175–6. The original census reports included only the total number of minorities and those groups that are over one million in number. This Soviet source lists all of China's minorities, explaining that the 1953 data were supplemented with 'subsequent, more precise official information on certain minority groups'. Excluded from the table are 200,000 Kaoshan who are located on Taiwan. Most sources list the Chuang at 6,611,000, thus increasing the 'other' category to just under one million.

[2] *Ten Great Years* (Peking: 1960), pp. 9–10. Some minorities are known to be located in other provinces even though source does not so indicate. The great majority, however, live in provinces listed.

hundred thousand continue to live as distinct groups in a few isolated areas of Heilungkiang province. Their language is almost extinct, and they are indistinguishable from the Han in appearance and culture. Even if some of them are aware of their ancestral background, it is not possible that nearly two-and-a-half million would, without prompting, report themselves as Manchus.

Does religion identify a national minority? In most cases the answer is negative. Nevertheless, the 1953 census listed 3·5 million Hui as a separate group within the Chinese society. The Hui, however, are simply Chinese of Moslem faith. Although the Hui did have some non-Chinese ancestry stemming from the Arab sea traders who intermarried with the people they proselytized, the number of these Arabs was relatively small and not significantly reinforced after the initial contacts during the seventh to thirteenth centuries. Since they are indistinguishable from the Han in their physical characteristics, many of the young Hui probably are succumbing to the antireligious pressures of the Communists, abandoning the faith of their parents and joining the Han majority. Thus the chances are that the number of Hui in China is actually decreasing.

While on the subject of assimilation, it must be taken that the process is accelerating under the Communist regime among other groups, too. Improvements in communications, greater mobility of individuals, expanded educational facilities which bring more minority children into Chinese middle and higher educational institutions, migration of large numbers of Chinese into minority areas, all make for assimilation whether by choice, by marriage or merely by proximity. Because the basic population figures for the minorities are already so fragile, the question of assimilation is significant not from a demographic viewpoint but rather as a social and cultural phenomenon. It must be kept in mind, however, that any 'normal' population count would make a special point of searching out and identifying some of the borderline minorities such as the Hui, thus presenting a somewhat unrealistic picture of the size of the group and its distinctiveness in the society.

In view of the factors mentioned above and due to the absence of any comprehensive statistics since 1953, projection of the 1953 figures on nationalities is not attempted. It is possible, however, to present some general idea of the trends in the vital rates among the minority populations.

One indisputable fact should already be apparent: there is no single rate of growth which can be applied across the board to the minority groups in China. Ranging from almost primitive mountain tribes to groups that are as advanced as the Han, their respective birth and death rates vary accordingly. The periodic sanitation drives and the expanding health facilities which caused a gradual drop in the death rate in most of China probably by-passed or were at least delayed many years for many millions of minorities in the low-density, isolated areas of the country. Periodic civil disorders also must have resulted in uneven losses among the minorities. The high birth rates that were prevalent among them – generally higher than among the Chinese – must have persisted at least through the 1950s, especially since the birth control policy initiated by Peking specifically exempted them from the campaign. Many of the groups probably still continue to reproduce at an unrestricted rate.

The combination of high fertility and mortality, as well as creeping assimilation and even flight, probably held down the increase among the minorities. Assuming therefore a nominal annual growth rate of one per cent, it is estimated that by 1970 the minority population of China was approximately forty-two million, comprising only slightly more than five-and-a-half per cent of the country's population. Actually, a precise rate-of-growth estimate is of little consequence. What is important is that the minorities have been increasing at a lower rate than have the Han. Clearly the trend evident over the past several decades will continue and the proportion of minorities to the Han in China will slowly but surely grow ever smaller.

Parenthetically, it should be noted that the Han themselves are by no means homogeneous, and marked differences in physical characteristics and temperament exist between the people of north and south China. The most important difference, however, is one of language. Mandarin speech prevails in northern China; in the south, particularly in the coastal provinces, there is great complexity of languages or dialects, many of them mutually unintelligible. What binds the Chinese together in this respect is not the spoken language but their written language – an ideographic script which represents ideas rather than sounds and can be comprehended by persons who cannot speak to each other.

The Chinese Communists were well aware, as were their predecessors, of the handicap inherent in the multiplicity of spoken, mutually unintelligible dialects and a written language that has no alphabet. After due consideration and study, Peking decided that the abandonment of

Table 12: Non-Han language groups and dialects of China

Southern China (*a*) *Miao-Yao group and Li*

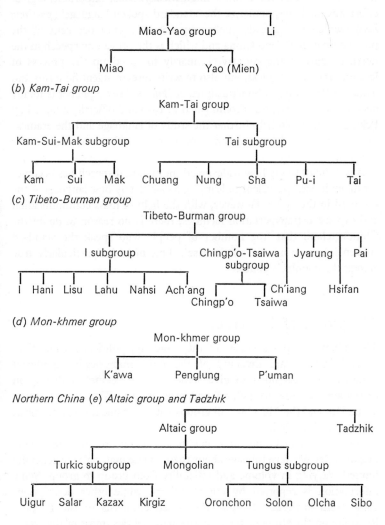

(*b*) *Kam-Tai group*

(*c*) *Tibeto-Burman group*

(*d*) *Mon-khmer group*

Northern China (*e*) *Altaic group and Tadzhık*

Source: Adapted from Chang Kun, 'National Languages', *Linguistics in East Asia and South East Asia,* Vol. II of *Current Trends in Linguistics,* edited by Thomas A. Sebeok (The Hague: Mouton & Co., 1967), pp. 161–2.

Chinese characters would not only divorce China from her past, but would also threaten national unity. Instead, several other approaches were tried to unify the country linguistically. Most important, a great effort was made to popularize the 'standard spoken language' (*pu-t'ung hua*) – which was already spoken by about seventy per cent of the population of mainland China and which is the prevailing speech in the northern part of the country. Primarily to speed up the process of learning the *pu-t'ung hua*, but also to write foreign scientific terms and names, a Romanized phonetic alphabet (*pinyin*) (any alphabet is totally alien to the Chinese) was promulgated in 1956 and officially adopted by Peking in 1958. To help further the study of language and the eradication of illiteracy, Chinese characters were simplified and made easier to learn.

It is difficult to say how widespread the standard speech has become; for many it was equivalent to learning a completely new language – one not used in the home. However, with the help of mass communication and expanded transportation facilities, there is no reason to doubt the Chinese claim that 'the number of people who speak the standard spoken language is ever on the rise'. This must be particularly true among the country's youth.

The pattern of differences

The following brief sketches of the economy, political organization, general culture and diversity of the most numerically significant minorities are intended to give some idea of Peking's difficulty in implementing minority policies and programmes. With the exception of the Hui and the Manchus, all groups with over one million people as of 1953 are included.

Since systematic ethnography in China is of fairly recent date, having begun under Western tutelage about 1920, source materials are generally limited, varying in volume and reliability from group to group. Some information is reported by ethnographers, while other descriptions come from amateurs. Despite the stated emphasis of the People's Republic on the study of the minority nationalities, most of the works published since 1949 are of little substance, being devoted largely to eulogies of the new government's attitude towards the minority groups and to diatribes against the Kuomintang's treatment of them. It is therefore difficult to assess any changes which may have occurred in the lives of these peoples. Although pervasive, Communist influence varied not only from group to group but also within groups. The smiling faces of minority youths sitting atop a new tractor in a Chinese magazine may, in fact, reflect some of the real changes that have taken place on the particular model commune, but it is quite possible that less than a hundred miles away peasants have experienced only minor changes in the traditional ways of living and working. Thus, the past and present tenses used in the following descriptions may perplex the reader; the reason for this confusion is simply the absence of more recent data which would provide the transition from the historical to the current scene. In general, however, the assumption is made that, lacking evidence to the contrary, the general pattern of living has changed little over the years.

The Chuang

The Chuang, known also as the Pien-jen, Nung-jen and T'u-jen, constitute the largest (see table 11) of the ethnic minorities in China. They are found for the most part in western Kwangsi, in the Wen-shan Special District in Yunnan and in a few scattered locations in Kwangtung and Kweichow. Because of their more advanced culture and considerable assimilation into the Han population, the true identity of the Chuang is vague, but they are thought to be genetically related to the Thai.

The general economic position of the Chuang has always been sounder than that of most of the other ethnic minorities of China. Before the Communist land reform, many Chuang owned the land which they cultivated; some were also landlords to Miao and Yao farmers. The Communists reapportioned much of the land, however, and by 1957 it was officially reported that more than ninety-five per cent of the farm households were members of agricultural cooperatives.

The Kuei-hsi Chuang Autonomous Chou, in which the majority of the Chuang live, is a fertile area rich in natural resources. About seventy per cent of the *chou* is heavily forested, and the timber is suited to industrial use. The principal economic activity is agriculture and the crop rice; tung and aniseed oil, bananas and mushrooms are also important commodities. The agricultural productivity of the area has reportedly been increased by irrigation projects; and although for the most part previously unexploited, its mineral resources (lead, manganese and iron) have also been undergoing some development.

The religion of the Chuang is similar to that of the other ethnic minorities of southern and south-western China and to the traditional beliefs of the Chinese themselves. They venerate the souls of their ancestors and believe in the spiritual influence of animate and inanimate objects. They consider that man's welfare is directly controlled by the spirit world and hold that certain individuals are given the power to manipulate these spiritual forces.

Historically, the language of the Chuang is a division of northern Thai. The classic Chuang language has no written form, however, and during the past few hundred years the Chuang people have increasingly used the Cantonese dialect – one indication of the degree of their assimilation. In the mid 1950s the Language Institute of the Chinese Academy of Sciences reportedly devised a system of writing the Chuang language. It is impossible to judge to what extent the system may have been accepted and used.

Besides speaking, reading and writing Chinese, the Chuang intermarry with and prefer to be identified as Han. It is frequently said (as of the Hui) they are not easily distinguishable from the Han; it is therefore surprising to find that the 1953 census lists 7,030,000 Chuang.

The Uighurs
The Uighurs reside principally in the Sinkiang Uighur Autonomous Region in western China, an area of great mountains and rivers, rich in mineral resources. Genetically, the Uighurs combine Europoid and Mongoloid characteristics. Prior to their coming to the Tarim Basin in Sinkiang Province a thousand years ago, the Uighurs were nomads. Because of the natural environment and their contact with the Chinese, however, they became sedentary agriculturists. This change in the economic pattern resulted in the disintegration of the characteristic clan and tribal system. Since the development of the new economy, the chief occupations of the Uighurs have been agriculture, horticulture and animal husbandry. Cotton is grown as a cash crop. White wheat and corn products are the basic foods of the Uighur; mutton is the most frequently eaten meat; raisins and melons are freely available. Mare's milk is drunk fresh and is also processed. Before the economic reforms of the Communist government, most of the land was owned by a few families. Farmers worked these lands on an equal-shares basis. Now they share their production with the state.

The extended family unit, found among most of the ethnic groups of

China, does not exist among the Uighurs. As they have neither clan nor tribal organization, the immediate family is the only social unit to which the individual feels any loyalty or attachment. Although polygamy is now nonexistent, there is a stigma attached to small families; the Uighurs, consequently, continue to maintain a high birth rate. The tactics which may have provided some success in reducing the birth rate of the Han could only have had minimal effect among the Uighurs. Nevertheless here, as in all minority areas, the Communist Chinese have instituted political cadres for the purpose of instilling extra-familial and extra-communal concepts of patriotism and citizenship.

Islam is the formal religion of the Uighurs, although they are not strict in the observance of ritual practices and characteristics of the old animistic religion remain. Belief in witches, ghosts, spirits and the like are merged with the more formal Islamic code, and there are superstitions attached to almost all objects whether animate or inanimate.

The Arabic script is used, but because of the high rate of illiteracy the abundance of literature traditionally found among the Turkic peoples is largely absent. The Uighurs speak Eastern Turkish (Uighur), a Turkic branch of the Ural-Altaic family, and regional variations of this language are insignificant.

The Yi

This minority group, known variously as the Yi, Lolo, Losu and Nosu, was reported at 3,254,000 in 1953 and is concentrated in the Liang-shan Yi Autonomous Chou in south-western Szechwan. These people are also found in western Kweichow, in eastern Szechwan and in northern Yunnan.

Parochialism is furthered by the mountainous nature of the territory and by the widely scattered villages; historically the Yi seldom identify themselves with any group other than the local settlement. This regionalism naturally results in varying forms of economic organization within the society. Prior to Communist Chinese control, landowners in Yunnan had certain administrative and political jurisdiction over the tenant farmers. In the Liang-shan region, the economy was traditionally based on slavery – captives gained through raids resulting from the extensive interclan vendettas. Peking, however, has announced the abolition of slavery and the redistribution of some of the land to the former slaves.

The pattern of warfare so prevalent within the Yi society was also an

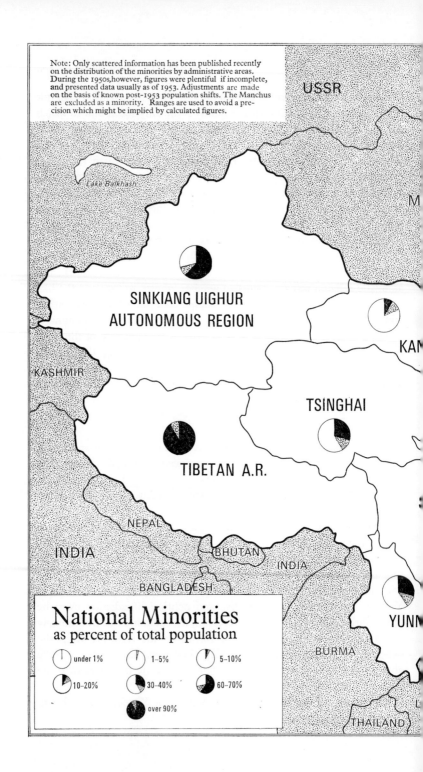

Note: Only scattered information has been published recently on the distribution of the minorities by administrative areas. During the 1950s, however, figures were plentiful if incomplete, and presented data usually as of 1953. Adjustments are made on the basis of known post-1953 population shifts. The Manchus are excluded as a minority. Ranges are used to avoid a precision which might be implied by calculated figures.

USSR

Lake Balkhash

M

SINKIANG UIGHUR
AUTONOMOUS REGION

KAN

KASHMIR

TSINGHAI

TIBETAN A.R.

NEPAL

INDIA

BHUTAN

INDIA

BANGLADESH

YUNN

National Minorities
as percent of total population

- under 1%
- 1–5%
- 5–10%
- 10–20%
- 30–40%
- 60–70%
- over 90%

BURMA

THAILAND

USSR

Lake Baikal

HEILUNGKIANG

LIA

KIRIN

INNER MONGOLIAN A.R.

LIAONING

Sea of Japan

NORTH KOREA

GSIA

.R.

HOPEI

SHANSI

SOUTH KOREA

SHANTUNG

Yellow Sea

SHENSI

HONAN

KIANGSU

JAPAN

ANHWEI

HUPEI

CHEKIANG

East China Sea

VAN

HUNAN

KIANGSI

WEICHOW

FUKIEN

Formosa Strait

TAIWAN

KWANGSI
CHUANG A.R.

KWANGTUNG

Hong Kong (British)
Macao (Port.)

RTH
NAM

Gulf of Tonkin

South China Sea

HAINAN

PHILIPPINES

integral part of relationships between the Yi and the Chinese. Yi raids
on Chinese villages were commonplace. To rid themselves of this
nuisance, many of these villages paid tribute to the Yi leaders. Once
this tribute relationship was established, the Chinese were allowed to
function in Yi society as merchants and even as landlords. The Yi
have traditionally maintained a dominant position in their association
with the Miao, who were frequently tenants on Yi land and who were
taxed and controlled politically by the Yi.

Agriculture and livestock breeding are the two main economic
activities of the Yi. There were many markets in which handicraft
products were bartered, and salt (which is imported) served as a medium
of exchange. The methods of tillage have probably changed little except
in those areas where close contact with the Chinese has been established.
The principal crop is rice; the staple diet of the Yi consists of food
prepared from rice, wheat, barley, millet, beef, mutton and pork.

The Yi society consists of the extended family unit, with all generations of males and their wives and children residing in the same household. For the Yi, human events are controlled by spirits which are
embodied in every object. These spirits, both good and evil, may be
propitiated through individuals known as *shaman* who apply mystic
interpretations to the spirit-problems at hand. Because the spirits cause
illness, crop failure and the like, the *shaman* act as doctors, priests and
weathermen. The language of the Yi is the Lolo-Nosu division of the
Tibeto-Burmese branch of the Sino-Tibetan family. A few individuals
specially important socially use a non-phonetic form of writing, but
the general population is illiterate and in the past considered writing
to be empowered with mystical attributes.

The Yi have little interest in distinguishing outsiders, categorizing
anyone who is not a Han or a Miao as a non-Yi, or simply as 'all others'.
This is typical for most of the peoples of rural inland China.

The Tibetans
Although probably ninety per cent of the Tibetans live in Tibet, there
are Tibetans – or groups so designated by the Chinese because of their
Tibetan culture – who are scattered in Szechwan, Yunnan, Tsinghai and
a few other provinces. Although the Tibetans have retained their cultural
identity largely through the bond of Lamaism (the Tibetan variant of
Buddhism), many of the local populations feel little identification with
the city of Lhasa, usually considered the focal point for all Tibetans.

Traditional Tibetan society comprised two general groups: the ecclesiastics and the laity, the latter being divided into nobility and commoners. Internal political control of the country was partly in the hands of a subgroup of the nobility, known simply as lay government officials, but church officials administered both religious and secular affairs and were the senior element in all public bodies. Because political and economic powers were in the hands of the same groups, the Communists initially attempted to convince the 'aristocracy' that no loss of these strengths would result from proposed socialistic reforms. Recognizing the powerful role of religion in Tibet, the Communists were cautious about changing the economic and political control of the monasteries.

The turning-point probably occurred in March 1959 when the Dalai Lama fled to India. With his departure, the Communist Chinese immediately instituted a so-called democratic reform movement to neutralize landowners and the theocratic hierarchy, and to reindoctrinate the youth of Tibet away from Lamaism and Tibetan traditions. Thus gradualism was abandoned as a policy. The new approach apparently brought the desired results and the Communists declared the formal establishment of the Tibetan Autonomous Region on 1 September 1965. The precarious stability that had existed in Tibet for a few years vanished with the Cultural Revolution, which permitted new attacks by the anti-Chinese groups, this time in the name of Maoism.

The effects of Communist pressures on Tibet's social organization, especially during the past ten years, must have been significant. The most affected groups were the fifteen per cent or so of the population in monasteries and the small number of merchants and nobles in the towns of Tibet. Nevertheless, political, social and cultural activities of the Tibetans are so inseparably interwoven with their religious, Lamaistic life, that even now the Communists probably cooperate with some segments of the religious hierarchy to control the area.

The staple diet of the Tibetan is yak's meat, mutton, barley, flour, cheese and tea. Those who dwell in lower altitudes also have fruit and vegetables. The most frequent item in the Tibetan diet is a hot beverage composed of water, tea, salt, soda and soured yak butter. Monogamy, polygamy and polyandry were all common in Tibet. Polygamy was practised among the wealthy. Polyandry was found among the herdsmen and farmers and, where it held, the husbands were usually brothers. The existence of polyandry would seem to offer a contradiction to the large number of men in monasteries; however, in contrast to the more

H

familiar lifetime dedication of monastery residents, there is a relatively rapid turnover among Tibetan monks.

The Tibetan language is related to Burmese and falls into the Sino-Tibetan family. There has been an alphabet (derived from the Hindi) for the written version of the language since the seventh century.

The Miao

More than ninety per cent of the two-and-a-half million Miao in China are concentrated in the province of Kweichow; the remainder are found in small scattered groups in western Hunan, Kwangsi, southern Szechwan and Yunnan. There are several dozen names used to represent the myriad subgroups of this people, each representing a separate group with a distinctive socio-economic pattern. Two autonomous *chou* have been established to formalize the political identity of the Miao: East Kweichow Miao-Tung Autonomous Chou and South Kweichow Puyi-Miao Autonomous Chou.

The Miao engage chiefly in farming, practised by family units which live in small villages and work the surrounding lands. Their only other significant economic activity is the shipping and trading of produce along the Chinese rivers. Farming in this mountainous area is usually of the cut-and-burn variety, in which land is cleared by cutting the vegetation and burning the remaining cover. The land is abandoned after a crop or two and not used again for several years. The main crops are corn, millet, barley, kaoliang and beans, while rice is grown on the scarce level land and on terraces along river banks. Also included in the diet of the Miao are vegetables, herbs, pork, beef and dog meat.

Beyond the village, each with its own headman, the Miao have little political organization. Political control by both the Chinese and Yi is traditional, however, for the purpose of taxation, and in some instances for military service. Apparently there was little self-awareness of the individual or self-identification with his people. Because the Miao rent their land from the Chinese or from the Yi, their economic position has been unfavourable. The Communists apparently have not introduced land reform among this group nor has the policy to encourage national consciousness been stressed.

Shamanism is the chief religion of the Miao, who believe that all things are permeated with mystical force which affects human life and that the unseen world of gods, demons, ghosts and ancestral spirits is primarily responsive to the manipulations of the shaman. The Miao, however, have no congregations or group worship services. Their language is a division of the Miao-Yao branch of the Sino-Tibetan family. Many of the numerous dialects are mutually unintelligible. Although there is no written form, in those areas where the Miao come in contact with the Han they read and write Chinese.

The Miao are characterized by local cultural variations which are greater than among any other non-Chinese ethnic group. Because of the mountainous terrain in which they reside, contact between villages is slight. Each village tends to develop traits and patterns peculiar to itself, and those which are nearer to Chinese or Yi communities undergo even further differentiation from those less close.

The Mongols

The majority of the Mongols are found south of the Amur river and north of the Yalu in Inner Mongolia, and in the provinces of Heilung-kiang, Kirin and Liaoning. Smaller numbers are dispersed throughout Kansu, Tsinghai and Sinkiang. The Mongols of China are closely related in language and culture to those of the Mongolian People's Republic, but the old political and military contacts between various tribal associations no longer exist and only some social and cultural tendencies remain.

For hundreds of years the economy of the Mongols was based almost exclusively on herding sheep, goats, cattle, horses and (in the western areas) camels. Despite some Mongol resistance, communes and state farms have been widely introduced in Inner Mongolia by the Communists. The number of Mongols working in agriculture and even in industry has also been gradually increasing.

The basic social unit is the extended family, a group comprising three or four generations which in the past operated independently of or in voluntary cooperation with other family units in the village. Private ownership of property has never existed in any of the Mongol societies; livestock has been the property of the kinship group and agricultural and grazing lands have been under the jurisdiction of the entire community.

Absence of individual ownership aided the colonization of Mongolian territory by the Chinese in the first years of the twentieth century and later. Trading on the custom that land was public domain, Chinese officials began to develop the legal fiction that although land was publicly owned, it did not belong to a Mongol nation, tribe or prince, but rather to the Chinese nation. The communist programme of communalizing agricultural land has followed the earlier general pattern of acquisition. The problems of political penetration were intensified by the usual conflict between the farmers (Han) and the herders (Mongols).

There has always been in the Mongol community a concept of public duty and obligation to higher political or military authority. This concept has been continually reinforced both under the Kuomintang and the Communists. Service in civil posts, military duty, payment of taxes and availability for corvée work are well-established patterns throughout the Mongol society.

Lamaistic Buddhism is the principal religion of the Mongols but encompasses many aspects of the indigenous shamanistic beliefs which prevailed prior to its introduction. Unlike Tibet, however, there were no ecclesiastical land holdings in the Mongol society. The Mongols speak essentially the same language, with some phonetic differences. Although the Cyrillic script has been adopted in Outer Mongolia, on the Chinese side of the border the traditional Mongol script is still in use. Mongolian literature, by no means voluminous, is devoted almost exclusively to Buddhist and Confucian texts. Chinese script is used by scholars, particularly in nonreligious matters.

Perhaps one of the reasons Chinese pressure on the Mongols in Inner Mongolia has not been more severe is the competition between China and the Soviet Union for the goodwill and support of the independent Mongolian People's Republic – a contest the Chinese have clearly been losing.

The Puyi

The Puyi are found in south-central and south-western sections of Kweichow province. Their political existence has been recognized by the People's Republic of China in the formation of the South Kweichow Puyi-Miao Autonomous Chou. They are also known as the Chung-chia, T'u-jen, T'u-chia, Yi-chia and Shui-chia.

The Chinese have traditionally accepted the Puyi into their society. Contrary to the usual situation, the Puyi have been shopkeepers in Chinese villages and have even competed with the Chinese in examinations for government posts. The Puyi often deny their non-Chinese ancestry. Before the advent of political control by the People's Republic each village had a headman who collected land taxes, adjudicated civil matters and liaised with the Chinese magistrate.

The diet of the Puyi is based on meat (pork, beef, horse and dog), grain and vegetables. Since they live in a semitropical area, many fruits are also available. Their religion is a form of animism which is very similar to Chinese folk religion. The universe is considered to be motivated by spirits and demons which can and must be manipulated to preserve a compatible environment for human existence. As a group that has readily assimilated into Chinese communities, a number of Puyi have become Buddhists, while others influenced by Western missionaries have embraced Christianity.

They speak a dialect of the northern Thai division of the Sino-Tibetan family. Local variations in speech are not significant, and many Chinese words are included in the vocabulary. There has never been a natively-created written form of the language spoken by the Puyi, but for several centuries the more educated have been able to speak and write Chinese. In the mid 1950s the Central Academy for National Minorities announced that a script for the Puyi language was ready for adoption, but it is not known if the introduction of this script into the society was achieved.

The Koreans

Almost all the Koreans in China live in the north-eastern provinces. The greatest concentration is found in an area of approximately 1,200 square miles in Kirin Province, an area which is part of the Yen-pien Korean Autonomous Chou.

Koreans probably began to migrate into Manchuria during the early part of the seventeenth century and have continued to do so for three hundred years despite official Chinese restrictions and the prohibition of emigration by the Korean authorities. Economic necessity has always been a primary cause of Korean emigration; political unrest following Japanese annexation of Korea in 1910 added to this motivation. By 1931 there were about 800,000 Koreans resident in Manchuria, fifty per cent of whom were in the Chien-tao District in Kirin. While Chien-tao was the only area in which they constituted a majority, Koreans were found almost everywhere in Manchuria and no town of any size was without its Korean minority. Most of the in-migrant Koreans were rice growers and therefore did not compete directly with the Chinese farmers in this area.

The Korean culture is characterized by a relatively high degree of homogeneity. In Korea, regional cultural variations are slight; local divergencies in the spoken language, for example, are of less than dialectal range. This homogeneity persists in Manchuria where the Koreans, rather than intermingle with Chinese, settled in sparsely inhabited areas thereby maintaining their own identity. Well-defined social classes have little meaning for the Korean. Even the traditional distinction between the hereditary landowner and the small farmer or fisherman, which existed in the homeland, is not found in Chien-tao.

Customary living patterns and family system of the Koreans are being remodelled by the Communists via an intensive programme of economic and cultural reorientation. As among other minorities, one of the important moves in this direction is the encouragement of extra-familial groups based on age or occupation. The officially sponsored youth programme, for example, has been directed to effect a major transfer of loyalties away from the home.

Although the concepts of Buddhism and Christianity have been introduced to and in varying degrees accepted by the Koreans, the original native beliefs in spirits have never been obliterated. Animism is still found in rural areas where the farmer believes that contact with the spirit world is an effective method for the control of the forces of nature.

The classification of the Korean language has not been agreed on by linguists but, whatever its position, it is clearly distinguishable from any other used in Asia. The contemporary form of writing is an alphabet with ten vowels and fourteen consonant symbols. These symbols combine to form phonetic syllables which are a great deal simpler than the characters used by the Chinese, and their simplicity contributes to the higher literacy rate among the Koreans. Many Japanese words have been adopted into the Korean vocabulary, and many older Koreans are able to speak Japanese.

In summary, it seems safe to predict that Peking's schizophrenic relationship with the minorities will continue for some time, on the one hand exaggerating their numbers and emphasizing their distinctiveness, on the other hand resenting this distinctiveness and pressuring them into greater conformity under increasing Han controls. In general, however, the historical pattern should continue. In areas favourable to sedentary agriculture Chinese culture should gradually be absorbed and the cultural patterns of the minority people modified. Within the periphery of China (in such areas as Sinkiang, Inner Mongolia and

Tibet, where the economy continues to be of a pastoral-nomadic variety and where minorities continue to exist as distinct ethnic groups) the programme to inculcate Chinese culture can expect to meet greater resistance. In the long run, however, it is improbable that the minorities will be able to withstand the overpowering combination of Chinese culture and communism.

6 · Implications and consequences

China's aims may be wrapped in unfamiliar ideology and she may be trying to reach them by routes which seem circuitous to the outside world, yet they are basically identical to the goals of all national governments: the economic and social progress and well-being of the country's population. Some readers may disagree with this statement, but what is important is that in China, perhaps more than in any country, there is an intimate interrelationship between economic growth and improvements in social conditions and the size, rate of growth and characteristics of her population. In other words, whether the present regime will succeed or fail in its objectives will depend on how effectively Peking will be able to cope with a population that is now increasing by almost fifteen million every year.

This chapter primarily will address three questions: How has China been able economically to absorb her ever-growing manpower? How successful has she been in feeding her vast population? Have the internal problems associated with the balance between population and resources had any international implications?

The economics of China's manpower

Quantitative aspects
The universal problem of defining the labour force and determining who should be included or excluded is particularly difficult in an overwhelmingly rural economy where children, old people and women take part in a variety of labour-related activities either on a seasonal or a part-time basis. The situation is further complicated in China where so many students continue to work part-time, while army personnel are involved in a variety of construction and production activities which in other countries would usually be kept for civilian personnel. Thus,

the standard questions that are used in the West in compiling labour force statistics are not necessarily relevant to the Chinese environment.

The most complete employment data regularly collected by the State Statistical Bureau in the 1950s were limited almost entirely to workers and employees – individuals who received wages or salaries from the State (see table 13). Other figures on the labour force appeared only spasmodically and were seldom adequately defined. And in fact even the worker and employee series left many questions unanswered.

Table 13: Workers and employees, 1949 and 1952–8
(absolute figures in thousands)

| year | total | male | female | per cent of total | |
				male	female
1949	8,004	7,404	600	92·5	7·5
1952	15,804	13,956	1,848	88·3	11·7
1953	18,256	16,124	2,132	88·3	11·7
1954	18,809	16,374	2,435	87·1	12·9
1955	19,076	16,603	2,473	87·0	13·0
1956	24,230	20,964	3,266	86·5	13·5
1957	24,506	21,220	3,286	86·6	13·4
1958	45,323	38,323	7,000	84·6	15·4

Source: Ten Great Years (Peking: 1960), pp. 180 and 182. The year 1949 was, of course, in no sense typical and should not be considered a useful base for purposes of comparison. The figure for 1958 reflects the Great Leap Forward policies; the eighty-five per cent increase over the preceding year is to a large extent due to the reclassification of other segments of the labour force and the spurt in quasi-industrial activities in both urban and rural areas.

Although this group represented the nucleus of the urban labour force, there were also workers and employees in the countryside engaged in agricultural (state farms and forestry) and nonagricultural activities. Conversely there was a significant proportion of the urban labour force, such as handicraft and various service personnel, which did not fall into the worker and employee category. In most towns and cities there was also a segment of the population that was engaged in agriculture and therefore did not even belong in the urban labour force. The situation is admittedly bewildering, but if an approximation of the force were required, it would not be unreasonable to assume that, under 'normal' conditions, about fifty per cent of the urban population was

Table 14: Distribution of nonagricultural employment: 1952–8
(population in thousands)

branch of the economy	1952		1953		1954	
	number	%	number	%	number	%
total	36,752	100·0	39,116	100·0	39,750	100·0
Material production branches	30,200	82·2	31,954	81·7	32,310	81·3
Handicrafts and carrier services	7,364	20·0	7,789	19·9	8,910	22·4
Salt extraction	500	1·4	500	1·3	500	1·3
Fishing	1,336	3·6	1,404	3·6	1,472	3·7
Industry	5,263	14·3	6,121	15·6	6,370	16·0
Water conservancy	134	·4	198	·5	266	·7
Capital construction	1,048	2·9	2,170	5·5	2,100	5·3
Transport, posts and telecommunications	4,655	12·7	4,764	12·2	4,873	12·3
Trade and the food and drink industry	9,900	26·9	9,008	23·0	7,819	19·7
Nonproductive branches	6,552	17·8	7,162	18·3	7,440	18·7
Finance, banking and insurance	351	1·0	396	1·0	632	1·6
Services	443	1·2	452	1·2	461	1·2
Education	2,005	5·5	2,159	5·5	2,206	5·5
Medicine and public health (inc. traditional medicine)	1,041	2·8	1,142	2·9	1,245	3·1
Cultural affairs	92	·3	100	·3	108	·3
Government administration	1,523	4·1	1,698	4·3	1,598	4·0
Mass organizations	1,053	2·9	1,143	2·9	1,090	2·7
Urban public utilities	41	·1	69	·2	96	·2
Meteorology	3	—	3	—	4	—

in the basic labour force. Thus, at about the time the Great Leap got under way there were probably some forty to forty-five million persons in this force – excluding the marginal participation of children, old people and other groups periodically rounded up for special drives and

1955		1956		1957		1958	
number	%	number	%	number	%	number	%
3,864	100·0	39,366	100·0	39,667	100·0	56,867	100·0
1,258	80·4	30,808	78·3	30,953	78·0	47,918	84·3
8,202	21·1	5,780	14·7	6,560	16·5	1,465	2·6
500	1·3	500	1·3	500	1·3	700	1·2
1,540	4·0	1,500	3·8	1,500	3·8	2,000	3·5
6,121	15·7	7,480	19·0	7,907	19·9	23,734	41·7
261	·7	409	1·0	340	·9	1,360	2·4
1,935	5·0	2,951	7·5	1,910	4·8	5,336	9·4
4,876	12·5	4,103	10·4	4,417	11·1	5,823	10·2
7,823	20·1	8,085	20·5	7,819	19·7	7,500	13·2
7,606	19·6	8,558	21·7	8,714	22·0	8,949	15·7
704	1·8	677	1·7	621	1·6	400	·7
470	1·2	479	1·2	489	1·2	489	·9
2,168	5·6	2,542	6·5	2,542	6·4	3,127	5·5
1,347	3·5	1,628	4·2	1,908	4·8	2,160	3·8
116	·3	124	·3	124	·3	131	·2
1,576	4·1	1,748	4·4	1,698	4·3	1,183	2·1
1,096	2·8	1,215	3·1	1,184	3·0	1,281	2·3
123	·3	133	·3	133	·3	150	·3
6	—	12	—	15	—	28	—

Source: J. P. Emerson, *Nonagricultural Employment in Mainland China 1949–58*, Bureau of the Census (Washington: 1965), p. 128.

mass labour activities. Because of the intensified efforts to move the unproductive segments of the population out of the cities, particularly during the last couple of years of the last decade, it is likely that the proportion of the economically active population to the total urban population increased. Since at the present even the size of the urban population cannot be determined, it would be absurd to attempt an estimate of the urban labour force.

Table 14 presents the distribution of nonagricultural employment in China during the years for which some data were available. Although not directly relevant to this discussion, the information gives a good idea of the country's economic priorities as reflected in its manpower statistics. As in the case of all such work, other interpretations of the material are possible; it is nevertheless a product of careful analysis that considers all available sources.

As for estimating the size of the rural labour force, it too continues to be little more than an educated guess. From the nature, context and inconsistencies of the few figures reported for the late 1950s, it is evident that, as in the case of the urban population, the Chinese themselves possess only approximate figures on the number and characteristics of the rural manpower available to them. For example, in March 1960 it was reported that 'in the rural areas of our country there are a total of some 230 million full- and half-manpower units, including both men and women, or a little over 200 million full-manpower units'. Later the same year an official publication stated that 'rural labour power constitutes roughly one-third to two-fifths of the rural population of our country', yielding a labour force of anywhere from 180 to 220 million. Other figures were also reported – in some cases quoting the actual number of individuals, while in others using a series of factors to convert part-time workers into full-time labour units. Which of the two concepts was used in arriving at a particular figure is often a matter of conjecture. An additional problem involves the question of agricultural versus nonagricultural labour force in the rural areas. In the pre-Communist period most estimates showed that about three-fourths of the rural labour force was engaged in agriculture. What it is now is also a matter of speculation.

Considering the complexities just described, it is indeed fortunate that, within the present context, it is not really necessary to wrestle with a precise estimate of China's labour force. In terms of the economic pressure generated by China's population, it is quite sufficient to consider the approximate number of people who fall within the age groups which represent the potential labour force, the increment by which this number is increasing, and the policies adopted by the regime in their efforts to balance the supply and demand of manpower. We can arrive at the gross size of the population within the productive age groups by briefly considering the age and sex structure of the Chinese population.

Whereas the total population for 1953 is usually accepted and used, there is virtually unanimous rejection of the scanty age–sex figures officially released by the Chinese. The reason is not difficult to find: the census-takers were able to count heads but could not come up with realistic age statistics. Even without the intrinsic complications in the custom of reckoning a new-born baby one year old, it is most likely that the illiterate Chinese farmer could only guess at his correct age. Perhaps because the Statistical Office realized it was not getting figures which reflected true ages, the official census results never included the usual age–sex composition of the population in 5- or 10-year age groups. Instead, they reported the number of children in the 0–4 and 5–9 age groups; the population 18 years and above; the number of 'youths' (possibly persons in the 15–24 age group); the number of people over 100 years of age; and a few other odd cohorts. Later some unofficial age and sex breakdowns were published by individual Chinese authors, presumably on the basis of the 1953 census reports. The chances are that these figures were no more authentic than the partial figures published earlier, and to confuse the issue further the separately reported sex ratios were given for ages that did not coincide with the groupings given for the age distributions.

This absence of reliable age and sex statistics for China is expected. What is more distressing is the unsophisticated manner in which the Communists used the data. Because populations must follow certain natural laws, politically motivated adjustments of the incomplete officially released 1953 age and sex figures were not difficult to spot – especially since these very discrepancies were the focal point of the census-related propaganda. Probably the most obvious inconsistencies relate to the first two five-year cohorts. In order to show the improvements in health and reduction in infant mortality under the new regime, the figures showed a much smaller number of persons in the 5–9 age group (born prior to 1949) in comparison with those aged 0–4 (born since 1949). Improvements did occur, but more gradually than the Communists would have us believe. Similarly, to prove an immediate decline in female infanticide and neglect, the figures showed a significant deficit of girls only for the 5–9 age group – born before the Communists assumed power.

Table 15: Age and sex distribution: 1953[1]
(in thousands)

ages	both sexes	male	female
All ages	582,603	302,101	280,502
0 to 4	90,871	46,796	44,075
5 to 9	63,720	33,760	29,960
10 to 14	54,738	29,553	25,185
15 to 19	52,971	27,995	24,976
20 to 24	48,106	25,001	23,105
25 to 29	45,116	24,034	21,082
30 to 34	40,146	21,379	18,767
35 to 39	37,288	19,412	17,876
40 to 44	32,337	16,688	15,649
45 to 49	29,261	14,948	14,313
50 to 54	24,798	12,675	12,123
55 to 59	20,936	10,598	10,338
60 to 64	16,897	8,221	8,676
65 to 69	11,909	5,532	6,377
70 to 74	7,960	3,361	4,599
75 to 79	3,695	1,499	2,196
80 to 84	1,225	453	772
85 & Over	629	196	433

[1] J. S. Aird, *The Size, Composition, and Growth of the Population of Mainland China,* US Bureau of the Census, Series P-90, No. 15 (Washington: 1961), p. 81. Based on the measurement and minor adjustment of a population pyramid that appeared in *Jen-min pao-chien* (People's Health), Vol. 1, No. 5 (1 May 1959), p. 463. Alternative age-sex projections through 1986 may be found in: J. S. Aird, *Estimates and Projections of the Population of Mainland China: 1953–1986,* US Bureau of the Census, Series P-91, No. 17 (Washington: 1968).

A number of attempts have been made to derive an age–sex structure which would be consistent with the few figures made public from the 1953 census, and then to match the implied levels of fertility and mortality with a model life table. These are rather speculative exercises which need not concern us here. Instead, table 15 presents what comes closest to being an 'official' age–sex structure; it originally appeared in the form of a pyramidal chart in a 1959 health journal. Although it undoubtedly includes all the familiar deficiencies and irregularities, it is a picture of the Chinese population that adequately gives the broad interrelationships this discussion needs.

One of the basic economic obstacles in age structure for most over-populated developing nations holds for China: a relative deficiency of the adult population. This was true in old China, true in 1953, and it is still true in the 1970s. Whereas in the economically advanced countries the proportion of children under fifteen years of age usually ranges between twenty and twenty-five per cent of the total population, in China it was close to forty per cent in 1953 and probably is every bit as high as this now. The smaller number of old people does not basically alter this economically unfavourable age structure, which results in a much higher dependency ratio – the ratio between dependents and the potentially productive population. The common practice of utilizing child labour, particularly in the rural areas, theoretically lessens the burden of childhood dependency but actually is neither an efficient unit of labour nor an economically necessary one in a country with traditional rural underemployment. The handicaps of this un-favourable dependency ratio are further aggravated by the productivity factor. In a Western nation a proportionally larger manpower pool uses highly productive and efficient means by which to support a relatively small dependent population; China with its low per capita productivity must rely on the worker or the peasant to support a much larger non-productive population. Furthermore, although the lower Chinese life expectancy does not necessarily apply to the engineers and scientists, they, along with the skilled workers or any other specially trained individuals whose productivity may have been raised, have fewer years in which to 'repay' the society for the additional expense of training them, and, through their productivity, to contribute to the accumula-tion of goods and capital.

Another basic problem of even more immediate concern to the regime is the absorption of the natural increment of labour – a problem greatly inflated by the promulgation of the Marriage Law, which intended that men and women 'enjoy' equal status in marriage and in the labour force, and by subsequent policies designed to get women out of the home and into field or factory. The exact age at which an individual enters the labour force is only incidental in that the magnitude of the problem is not affected. In the early 1950s there were as many as ten million and in the late 1960s probably over fifteen million persons turning sixteen years of age every year. Feeding, clothing and educating these millions is a frightening undertaking. Because of the decrease in the labour force due to mortality, only a part of the sixteen-year-olds represent a growth increment; nevertheless, how does a nation, for generations experiencing underemployment and disguised unemployment, manage to absorb such youth effectively into the economy? How could this underemployment, sometimes estimated at as high as twenty-five per cent and in the past somehow absorbed within the close family unit, be handled under the new conditions in which the ability of the family to control its own destiny has all but disappeared? The trial-and-error approaches undertaken by the regime indicate this to be the exigency which has caused Peking more concern than the relatively simple pressure of population.

During the period of the middle 1950s, the Communists were quite candid about the surplus of manpower and the challenges it presented. Although official sources pointed out that 'the countryside is like a vast expanse of the sea in which the labour force is swallowed up', they nevertheless admitted that 'the unemployment problem is no less serious in the country than in the city'. And still, despite a gradual acceleration of the birth control campaign, the Chinese entered the First Five-Year Plan in 1953 quite confidently. Influenced by Western and Soviet experience, they must have concluded that to concentrate on the building of a modern industrial base, with all its implications and ramifications, would gradually draw off and utilize in the cities the excess rural manpower. Millions of persons did flock to the cities (see chapter 3), but the cities were not prepared to absorb them – not in terms of jobs, nor housing, nor food. This 'blind infiltration' was the first of a series of waves and trickles of migrants into the cities that have caused the regime perpetual problems of controlling the influx and moving out the excess manpower. Only relatively limited employment opportunities could be created in the cities during these early phases of industrialization and most of the manpower had to remain in rural China. The political turmoil and economic activities associated with the creation of the mutual aid teams and later the agricultural cooperatives probably managed to keep the rural population occupied, although undoubtedly the pre-Communist underutilization of manpower must have continued.

The first major upheaval to cause drastic changes in the approach to labour utilization came about in 1958 with the announcement of the Great Leap Forward and the creation of rural communes. Intent on quickly becoming a world power, China abandoned the slow and steady Soviet-style methods of economic development, ceased all concern about surplus manpower and virtually overnight proclaimed a severe manpower shortage. Literally hundreds of reports appeared in the Chinese press describing the difficulties encountered in all segments of the national economy. A nation-wide campaign was initiated to mobilize every available pair of hands for some form of productive labour. Through the establishment of dining halls, vast child-care centres and other cooperative facilities for mending clothes, cleaning houses and performing other domestic chores, millions of women were 'liberated' from housework for full-time work in the factory or field. Because the new agricultural techniques relied primarily on the most intensive type of labour utilization, the manpower shortage became particularly severe in the rural areas. Three of the eight basic requisites for agricultural production – deep-ploughing and soil improvement, fertilization and irrigation – were especially significant from the viewpoint of labour input. One need not accept at face value the reported figures (all of which were exaggerated during the Great Leap), but they are nonetheless most indicative of the labour utilization policies during that period. For example: 'One hundred million persons have been mobilized to participate in the deep-ploughing movement', 'Ninety million peasants are engaged in collecting manure and moving it to the fields', 'Seventy-seven million persons were engaged in water conservation projects'. Additional millions were engaged in attempts to increase the acreage under cultivation, in planting 'forty billion' trees along railways and highways and in villages, and so forth.

Of particular significance in terms of labour utilization was the creation of commune industries. Because of the prestige value associated with nonagricultural work, village industry was a fairly popular novelty, and local cadres concentrated large quantities of resources and manpower for its construction and operation. They were encouraged by the party's frequent proclamations that industry is the key to China's future. The fiasco of the backyard furnaces for the production of iron and steel is well known. As many as fifty million persons were reportedly involved in this effort of producing low-grade, unusable steel at an excessive cost. Another five million full-time workers were employed in a variety of other commune industries that came into being during the Great Leap.

The excesses of that era had their inevitable effects. A 1957 survey showed that ninety per cent of the time spent by the peasants in production was devoted to agricultural and subsidiary production. By 1960 a drastic change had occurred in the occupational distribution of the rural labour force. It was reported that only a little over fifty per cent of the manpower was actually engaged in agricultural production and that the labour shortage was due primarily to the increased number of workers in nonagricultural activities such as local industry, capital construction and communications. With all due respect to the hardworking Chinese women, the labour problem was aggravated by the fact that it was primarily the men who were drawn off into the nonagricultural mass projects, while the newly 'liberated' women became the major manpower source in agriculture. This inefficient and wasteful use of rural manpower coinciding with some of the worst weather of several decades resulted in a breakdown of agriculture and in the most severe food shortage so far experienced by the Chinese people under the Communist regime.

The Great Leap Forward turned out to be an economic disaster, but it may have been a blessing in disguise in terms of the practical and painful lessons it taught on the utilization of the country's manpower. For in theory there was nothing wrong with the effort to involve the masses in some form of productive activity; there was nothing wrong with the attempt to bring industry to the surplus rural manpower. The error was in the way the policies were implemented. China's labour supply was very elastic, but not elastic enough to accommodate the unbelievable excesses practised during the Great Leap. That the Communists benefited from the experiences of the late 1950s is evident from some of the policies introduced during the next decade.

The most important post-Leap change in China's policies was a shift in economic priorities, resources and manpower to agriculture and to those industries (such as fertilizer factories and agricultural equipment plants) which support agriculture. Nonessential commune industries were discontinued and the press and radio daily pronounced that 'agriculture is the foundation of our economy'. The economic depression in the urban areas led to reduced production and in the complete closing of many of those industries which relied on agriculture for their raw materials. Because of these depressed conditions in China's cities, the regime undertook what seemed to be the most successful effort to reduce the size of the urban population. Every extra person in the city was considered to be a burden on the economy and millions 'volunteered' to move back to the countryside. It was determined that the labour necessary for any future industrial expansion should be drawn primarily from the labour reserves already in the cities. What then could be done with these additional millions now that the excesses of the rural manpower were once again the responsibility of the countryside?

To cope with the rural manpower problem and at the same time to bolster the country's rural economy, the regime supplemented basic agriculture by introducing a major national policy to diversify agricultural operations and to increase subsidiary production. In the sense that it also was intended to put every available pair of hands to work, the approach was somewhat similar to that followed during the Great Leap, but Peking no longer predicted any grandiose results; the main objective apparently was to get people into any possible productive activity with only secondary concern about labour efficiency and productivity. The new policy therefore differed in one major respect: agricultural production took precedence over all other activities, and subsidiary production was only to be pursued if basic production would not be affected.

Diversification of rural operations was carried out on two parallel tracks. The first pertained to the household itself and, in a sense, was an extension of the private plot approach which once again was returned to the peasant. Children, old people and others not suitable for collective labour were expected to concentrate their efforts on subsidiary production which could be pursued in and around the house. For example, they could plant and care for fruit trees and bamboo around their homes, raise household animals and fowl, engage in weaving, sewing and embroidering, as well as in collecting, hunting and fishing. Although the additional output of each household would presumably be slight, multiplied by some 120 million households the total would not only serve rural needs but also help provide additional food and consumer goods for the cities.

The second track of the diversification effort of the middle 1960s involved collective efforts of the commune. As during the Great Leap, the activities in this category included irrigation and water conservation projects, reclamation of previously unused lands, particularly in the mountain regions, afforestation, and other efforts that would require mass labour and higher-level planning and organization. Increased breeding of livestock was also greatly encouraged. It is a source of fertilizer; it represents 'labour power' (draught animals); it furthers light industry (furs, skins, meat, milk, eggs), which in turn requires support from heavy industry; and finally, 'with the development of husbandry, a large amount of labour force can be absorbed'. The distinction between the mass projects at this time and those during the Great Leap was that manpower now could be drawn off from agriculture only during the slack season.

To implement this policy of labour utilization, which continued until the Cultural Revolution in the summer of 1966, the Communists provided an inducement. The incentive was nothing other than profit. The party realistically admitted that whether the farmer would be willing to produce certain subsidiary products 'would be determined by the existence of marketing possibilities', and one of the reasons given for expanding subsidiary production was that it 'increases the cash income of the peasants and further improves the lives of the peasants'. To make sure that the products of diversified operations found an outlet, not only was the rural marketplace once again legalized, but much of the responsibility for subsidiary activities on the commune was given to the supply and marketing cooperatives which in some areas organized teams to travel around the countryside buying up products either grown or made by the peasants.

The rapidity with which China emerged from her economic trough – despite many predictions that she would never come up for air again – indicates the regime must have been doing something right. Although the Communists could not publicly admit it, that China 'bounced back' was in large measure due to the leaders' appreciation of what makes the Chinese peasant produce. Peking gave the peasant adequate incentives and by the mid 1960s the recovery of the Chinese economy was evident in both city and countryside. Industrial growth once again pulled millions into the urban areas – many of them workers and employees who had been sent 'down to the countryside' during 1960 and 1961. During this period, however, the regime never lost sight of the philosophy that, if the economy is to continue to progress, agriculture must receive top priority. Looking back, in terms of our primary concern, it seems that the policies adopted during the 1960s did succeed in at least limiting the difficulties of labour utilization.

With the onset of the Cultural Revolution in 1966 the country went into another cyclical economic turnround. The attack focused specifically on the introduction of incentives after the Great Leap. The word 'economism' came into the Chinese lexicon, the leadership contending that 'power-holders' were using material incentives to corrupt the 'revolutionary masses'. As a result, in the urban areas wages were reduced, material incentives were eliminated, 'spiritual' incentives were substituted, and severe personnel cuts were made in government agencies and enterprises. In the rural areas the Mao faction condemned the 'monstrous crimes' of Liu Shao-ch'i, the 'Number one party person in power taking the capitalist road', for extending the concept of private plots and free markets, and for increasing the number of small enterprises which were solely responsible for their own profits and losses. Thus the relatively free rural economy that had crept into being was once again suddenly terminated by the advent of the Cultural Revolution.

The major disruptions caused by the Cultural Revolution, the battles of the Red Guards, the attacks on the Communist Party, the Army's emerging role, and finally the efforts to brake the revolution are all part of the record now. What concerns us in the aftermath are its effects on manpower utilization.

The economic policies during and immediately after the Cultural Revolution were frequently compared to the Great Leap Forward of 1958, particularly because workers throughout China were being exhorted to outdo each other in a new 'industrial emulation campaign', and peasants were asked to contribute more and more time and effort for mass projects. Despite the Chinese press acknowledgment that women have 'special characteristics' (narrow-mindedness, inferiority feelings, low political and technical ability, all of which manifest themselves in a preference for home and family), there was nevertheless a continuous pressure on Chinese women to 'take a vigorous part in socialist revolution and construction'. Through perpetual study of Mao's writings and sayings, the Chinese people were to be transformed into a new breed of supermen and women who would go on to build a new society and, eventually, a new world.

The Cultural Revolution was meant to purify Chinese ideology. Although an effort was made by Mao and his collaborators to maintain economic production, because the Revolution called for some drastic economic changes and the Red Guards got out of hand, production did once again suffer a significant setback in the form of work-stoppages, shortages of raw materials and disruptions of transportation facilities. With the slowdown in factories, the closing of most educational institutions, and the dismantling of the technical bureaucracies which had supervised urban enterprises and maintained certain fiscal and technical standards, China once again found itself with a surplus of urban man-power. The exact number of urban dwellers who were moved to the countryside cannot be determined: estimates vary from as low as five to ten million, to twenty-five million, to as many as 'one-third of the urban population'. What was the object in moving millions of people – the overwhelming majority of them educated and skilled well above the average peasant – out of the cities? How was the countryside to absorb them in such a way that their training and experience (already in short supply in China) would not be wasted? The answer lay in a blending of something old and something new into fresh approaches to China's economy and manpower utilization.

The new economic course set out for the People's Republic continued the emphasis on agricultural development. It was to be stepped up, however, by establishing a network of small supportive industries, based largely on local resources but also drawing on talent and equip-ment from major urban industries. Peking admits that the country is 'limited in funds, resources, techniques, equipment, and other condi-tions' for the development of large industries, but 'can take full advan-tage of various scattered limited local resources so that they can produce with what is locally available and sell their products in local markets in order to cut down shipping costs'. In theory, at least, this approach would build up the purchasing power of the vast rural population, raise the level of self-sufficiency at every administrative level from commune to province, and help to accumulate capital for the develop-ment of heavy industry at some later date. At a time when relations with the Soviet Union were at their worst, China added urgency to the construction and dispersion of local industries by holding a threat of war as a distinct possibility: 'Be prepared against war, be prepared against natural disasters, and do everything for the people.'

Much of the above rationale may be valid but it is not complete. In proposing birth control, the Communists rarely if ever mention the economic burden resulting from a high birth rate; in introducing small local industries they refrain from discussing what may well be the most important reason for dispersing industry in the rural areas – manpower absorption. The closest they come to admitting the existence of this problem is with almost incidental statements, such as that running industries by the masses 'fully utilizes local manpower'.

According to the most recent information, the Chinese countryside has indeed become an active economic producer. It may not contribute significantly to the production of steel, coal or electronic equipment, as claimed by Peking, but the local industries are important in equipping and supporting agriculture and in supplying the daily necessities of the rural population. In many instances local industries may be little more than workshops, but they seem to provide rural China with an ever larger share of its requirements for such products as chemical fertilizers and cement, farm machinery and implements, generators and transformers, and, perhaps most important, spare parts, the supply of which has always presented a major obstacle to even a limited mechanization of the countryside. Millions of peasants, young and old, supplemented by other millions of recent urban migrants, are busy building or working in these small factories and workshops.

From the Western point of view these local industries may seem inefficient and even wasteful, but there is no lack of jobs and from the Chinese point of view even the lowest level of labour productivity appears worthwhile because the alternative is no productivity at all on the part of a large segment of the population. Mao Tse-tung does not believe in the old theory which contends that by developing heavy industry the benefits will eventually be diffused throughout the society. It matters little whether the motivating force is contingency or philosophy; he is willing to sacrifice a more rapid economic growth by building the economy from the bottom up. He rejects the profit motive and tries to substitute enthusiasm and energy inspired by selflessness and a unity of purpose. How successful he will be in changing human nature is anyone's guess. To what extent he will be able to convince the youth that, for the good of the Chinese nation and people, their future lies in productive work in the countryside is questionable. But for the time being, China's population and manpower absorption problems have been funnelled into the rural areas and (one might even say) solved there.

Qualitative aspects
The preceding discussion concentrated on manpower absorption with little regard to the qualitative aspects involved. And yet the quality of a nation's labour resources – the educational attainment and existing skills – has a direct bearing on the problems of labour utilization and, consequently, on the goals a nation can set for itself. In urban areas the

correlation between the number of qualified workers and industrial development is obvious; it is perhaps less evident but just as true in the countryside, where an uneducated peasant represents a proven handicap to the introduction of new methods and techniques into agricultural production.

In China the trained urban élite was small indeed; the peasants, although industrious and persevering, were still for the most part illiterate. Because the Communists were well aware that education must accompany economic development, they placed it high on their list of priorities. But just how does a country establish an educational system with a potential enrolment of over 100 million students? The sheer magnitude of the undertaking staggers the imagination. The limited economic resources were enough of an obstacle. The Communists added another one: the small core of intellectuals (a catch-all term for persons with certain levels of education), although obviously vital to the successful expansion of the educational system, were considered politically untrustworthy and had to be purged periodically for real or suspected 'bourgeois deviationism'. For twenty years now the Communists have been wrestling with the requirements of quantity, quality and political purity in education and have both significant achievements and painful failures to show for their efforts.

In education, as in all activities in China during the first few years under the new regime, the major emphasis was on reorganization, reorientation and consolidation. A basic educational reform in 1951 called for some changes in organization and the establishment of technical and specialized schools and colleges, stressed ideological 'correctness', and guaranteed everyone in the country an opportunity to obtain an education. The innovations during this period did not, however, depart from the basic pedagogical concepts pursued in Western societies. Enrolment soared and by 1957 millions of workers and peasants had gone through a variety of literacy courses; over sixty-four million children were enrolled in either the four- or six-year primary schools; almost eight million attended either the regular or the specialized secondary schools which ran anywhere from three to six years; and almost 450,000 were enrolled in the institutions of higher education with curricula that covered from two- to four-plus years.

The above figures represent a significant and undeniable achievement – but an achievement with predictable dilemmas and confusions. With some ten per cent of the state budget allocated for education by

1957, the cost was an obvious burden. The rapid growth in enrolment created an acute shortage of teachers which in turn resulted in a lowering of qualifications for teaching personnel and a fall in the quality of instruction. The situation was no better with regard to school buildings, equipment, textbooks and other paraphernalia necessary for the operation of reasonably efficient schools. In general, too much emphasis was placed on numbers and on the fulfilment and over-fulfilment of enrolment quotas, while not enough attention was paid to personnel and facilities, to quality and requirements, and to the synchronization of education with economic planning (a pre-requisite in all communist countries).

The ill-fated Great Leap Forward, which was launched in 1958 in order to transform China rapidly into an advanced industrial nation, brought about a number of drastic changes in the country's educational policies so that it could better reflect the new mood and the new requirements of the economy. Of the two schools of educational thought in evidence in China, these changes represented a temporary victory of one: the Mao school. One theory, presumably expounded by Liu Shao-ch'i, considered it wasteful to divert student energies into political and production activities and wanted instead to emphasize academic curricula and teaching methods in order to produce 'experts'. The other school, which got the upper hand in 1958, supported the 'red' part-work, part-study concept preferred by Mao – a system that would produce 'revolutionary successors' who would see no distinction between mental and physical labour and who would be politically correct. A directive issued by the Ministry of Education set down three basic principles of education: (1) it was to serve politics; (2) it was to promote production; and (3) in order to achieve these ends, it was to be under the direction of the Communist Party. All schools and universities established factories, farms, and other enterprises in which students joined in operating limited production facilities on a part-time basis. At the same time, communes, factories, and other institutions were made responsible for establishing and maintaining their own schools – including the costs of running them.

The new philosophy of integrating all education with production resulted in an even more rapid growth of enrolment and a still further deterioration in the quality of education. With shortages of teachers and facilities, and with the greatest emphasis placed on productive labour and political purity, only a relatively small segment of the student population was able to pursue their education without major disruptions.

The combination of natural calamities and mismanagement which forced a retreat from the Great Leap policies had parallel repercussions in the field of education. The educational system, expanded too rapidly, started to contract; substandard schools were closed, productive labour for students was relaxed, and by the 1961–2 school year much of the emphasis was again shifted to the serious pursuit of education, i.e. 'expertness'.

It was not an absolute rejection, however, of the Great Leap policies in education; rather it was a backward step to adjust for the excesses that denigrated the educational system over the previous few years. Soon it became evident that there were forces pulling the system in different directions. On the one hand, the educational system was asked to supply the state with revolutionary youth whose love of Mao and motherland would transcend all personal considerations, and to do this by emphasizing ideological education and physical labour for students, especially in the 'work-study' and 'farm-study' schools. On the other hand, official editorials in the *People's Daily* urged schools to implement 'the policy of less quantity and high quality to enable the students to assume more initiative and to be more lively and free in their studies, with a view to creating conditions for the overall development of students – morally, mentally and physically'. On the whole these contradictions seemed to result in a fairly balanced approach to education, and it was this middle road between quality and quantity that was followed by China until the start of the Cultural Revolution in mid 1966. China was 'walking on two legs'.

The slogan 'walking on two legs' is an important practical rationalization of many of China's problems. It says in effect that in her present stage of development, China is unable to use the best and most efficient methods of production and is unable to give the people all they might want in terms of goods and services. It is therefore necessary to strive toward objectives by using a variety of methods and diverse approaches, be they old or new, efficient or inefficient. The slogan is particularly applicable to the field of education where China up to the Cultural Revolution had indeed already been walking on two legs since the creation of the new regime. One leg of China's educational system was providing the masses with the rudiments of the three Rs, instilling in them a certain political awareness, and in some cases providing them with certain skills that would make them more productive workers. (Considering the great variety of schools and multiplicity of approaches, China has been walking on the legs of a centipede in this single sector of mass education.) The other leg of the system continued to cater (as it did in the pre-Communist period) for the more promising urban student, who was expected to enter one of the better institutions of higher learning and eventually rise to a key production, research, or administrative position in society.

On the whole, it must be admitted that Peking deserves a good mark in the general approach and achievements in education. Despite periodic disruptions and ventures into uncharted pedagogical waters, China has managed to create and operate a system quite suited to her conditions and goals. Because she was able neither to provide the hundreds of millions of people with a first-rate education nor to utilize a uniformly well-trained labour force, she advanced on 'two legs'. She encouraged an atmosphere of learning, made literacy among the masses one of the primary goals, managed to elevate the overall educational level of rural youth, and trained adequate numbers of middle-level specialists and technicians; at the same time she did not neglect the economy's requirements for higher-level professional personnel, particularly engineers and scientists. China consciously elected to emphasize the training of specialists, rather than those with a broad academic background. This was true at the higher education level where, in addition to those who completed the more comprehensive programmes in their fields, thousands of specialists graduated from two-year schools in engineering, medicine, economics and so forth. This emphasis was also true at the secondary level. Variously referred to as vocational, specialized or technical schools were set up at the secondary level to train youth in such fields as 'engineering', agriculture and forestry, public health, and finance and economics. Although after 1958 most of this type of training was taken over by production and service organizations running the work-study or on-the-job training programmes, the teaching of secondary-level specialists continued to be an important aspect of the Chinese educational system.

Over the years there have been known imbalances between the output of the educational system and the needs of the economy, but usually China has been able to adapt not only her education to the rising needs but also her needs to the available manpower. Undoubtedly there were shortages of persons with specific types of training or education. There were also periods, such as the early 1960s, when the depressed urban economy was unable to absorb all the graduates (particularly from the junior and senior secondary schools), forcing one of the periodic waves of deportations of youth to the countryside. Nevertheless, in the spring of 1966 when the Cultural Revolution began gradually to gain momentum, both China's economy and her educational system appeared to have returned to an essentially balanced and productive level.

Among the most important consequences of the Cultural Revolution has been its impact on China's educational system. Concerned about the built-in advantages enjoyed by the children of better-educated urban parents, and convinced that education once again was slipping away from the people to the professional teachers, technocrats and even party leaders with their bourgeois ideas, Mao declared in May 1966 that 'while [the students'] main task is to study, they should also learn other things; that is to say, they should not only learn book knowledge, they should also learn industrial production, agricultural production and military affairs. They should also criticize and repudiate the bourgeoisie.' To make sure that the ancient distinction between scholar and peasant, urban worker and farmer, would once and for all be obliterated, he closed China's schools – 'to carry the educational revolution through to the end' – and claimed the released students as 'little warriors of the Cultural Revolution', better known as Red Guards.

The essential reforms proposed by Mao at that time may be summarized briefly as follows: (1) abolish the old examination system to overcome the advantages which accrued to children from cultured and prosperous families; (2) shorten the curriculum at all levels of education and place much more emphasis on political indoctrination and military training; (3) integrate study with productive labour at all schools and all levels; and (4) eliminate all theoretical study and research which are not an integral part of a production effort. It was much easier to prescribe these reforms than to implement them.

Efforts to reopen schools were started as early as September 1967, but for all practical purposes they were unsuccessful. Youngsters who had experienced the freedoms and prestige of being Red Guards were unwilling to return to their classes; teachers were fearful of renewed attacks. Very gradually some of the schools unlatched their doors, but from all indications more time was spent in arguments and discussions as to what should be taught and how, than on actual studies. Additional time was taken by the task of writing new teaching materials to replace textbooks which had been rejected on the grounds that they allowed 'the foreign bourgeoisie to continue their dictatorship over the Chinese people'. Thus the process of reopening schools was spread over several years.

By the autumn of 1970, after a four-year suspension of most classes, the schools in China were in operation once again. The broad guidelines and general policies that came down from Peking were implemented, but since most of the decisions as to the nature and content of education were to be worked out at the local level it is impossible to describe the structure of the system that evolved, except in general terms. Curricula at all levels now stress the ideological and vocational, play down traditional academic training and, depending on the type and location of the school, include productive labour in field or factory. The length of study at the primary and secondary levels has been reduced throughout the nation, but because of continued experiment that takes into consideration 'actual conditions' within the local school districts, a great diversity exists. In some localities the six-year primary and six-year secondary schools have each been shortened by one year; in many areas primary and junior middle schools were merged into seven years of instruction, with senior middle schools (where available and on a selective basis) to provide an additional two years; some schools are experimenting with four years for both primary and middle school students; and undoubtedly other combinations are also being tried. Thus, where it is available, pre-university education may range anywhere from eight to ten years.

Entrance examinations for admission to institutions of higher education have in fact been abolished, and prospective college students must first have contributed several years to production and are now selected (often elected) from among the young workers, peasants and discharged soldiers. Following Mao's dictum, emphasis is on technical and scientific institutions, now closely associated with factories, mines and farms, and the term of study may range anywhere from one to three years. Many of these technical institutions were relocated from urban to rural areas. The humanities – history, philosophy, literature, economics, journalism and education – were singled out for special criticism and omitted from the curriculum as independent fields of study.

The political turmoil that took place during the Cultural Revolution, the verbal and literal battles between various factions all claiming Mao's support, the roles of the military and the decimated party machinery are usually beyond the comprehension of most casual readers of the Western press. Bewilderment is increased by the variety of interpretations presented by both reporters and professional observers of developments in China. It may be some time before the long-term validity of the current experiments in education can be assessed, but there is no doubt that the closing of schools for almost four years left a gap in the education of China's youth that may be difficult to close. Meanwhile, what effect have the recent policies had on the problem of manpower utilization and on requirements for trained manpower within the economy?

Just as during the Great Leap in 1958, there is now a boom of education because of the large proportion of the population involved in some form of part-time learning or training process. Since the Chinese Communists have a tendency to overdo any good thing, almost everyone could be termed a 'student', for every peasant is learning from the 'educated' youth sent down to the countryside and every urban-bred migrant is said to be learning from the peasants. Just how many people are now part of the educational system is impossible to say. Considering the decentralized controls and the multiplicity and variety of educational units, it is doubtful that any valid figures on the number of students at the various levels will become available for some time to come. It seems safe to conclude, however, that as a result of the Cultural Revolution there has been an improvement of education in the rural areas. Going hand-in-hand with the changes that have taken place in the economic sector of rural China (discussed earlier in this chapter), it is very likely that the manpower needs of rural production – both agricultural and industrial – can be met by the existing system. Since so much of the training seems to be little more than schools for apprentices, China should be able to increase its number of low-level technicians with a smattering of instruction in industrial and agricultural techniques.

Thus it seems quite possible that China has managed to concentrate all her manpower absorption problems into rural areas and, with her new economic and educational policies, may at last have found a long-term solution to them. It is not only the creation of local industries that should take up the manpower slack; if the theory is correct that a trained individual, be he worker or peasant, tends to create additional jobs, the Cultural Revolution certainly seems to have injected large enough numbers of 'intellectual' youth to stimulate additional manpower requirements and, optimistically, create a snowball effect.

The major remaining problem, of course, is in the urban sector, for it was this 'leg' of the educational system – the one that was responsible for the development of future generations of scientific, technical, and managerial skills necessary for modernization – that Mao amputated in 1966. It is very probable that as the schools settle down, some of the more specialized needs of the modern urban sector of the economy will be met by persons trained for two or three years in specialized urban colleges and broadened by their practical experience in a factory, mine, or other enterprise. But inevitably the end to training of truly professional scientists and engineers is bound to have long-term repercussions on China's abilities to compete in a world that every year becomes more dependent on technology. From all external evidence the present Peking leadership does not seem to be concerned. But for those not fortunate enough to have 'the faith', for those without the security provided by Mao's thoughts, the crucial question remains unanswered: how does China propose to replace her current top echelon of foreign-trained specialists with home-grown successors?

Food resources and population

Intimately related to her demographic predicament and inseparable from her future is China's ability to feed about one-fifth of the world's population on less than one-tenth of the world's cultivated land. Ancient historical records indicate that the Chinese had no problem in feeding themselves, gaining a reputation for being particularly skilled and hard-working farmers. Early travellers invariably commented on the great opulence of the country. As the population increased over the centuries and more and more forest was cut down to provide land for cultivation, the difficulties gradually mounted. Not only was there an ever-increasing demand for food, but the devastation of China's forests and grasslands sent millions of tons of soil into the rivers, depleting the earth of this rich topsoil, raising river beds, and causing ever more frequent and more disastrous floods. Thus, particularly in more recent times, it was only the twin reapers of famine and disease that kept China's population and food resources in reasonable balance.

This background and the rapid drop in mortality experienced in China since 1949 inspired many crystal-ball gazers to prophesy, on the basis of either their calculations or their prejudices, that China's food production could not keep pace with her population growth and there-fore the collapse of the Communist regime was imminent. But despite climatic and topographic handicaps that permit only a fraction of her land to be cultivated, despite many policies and programmes that at times were more destructive than beneficial, China continues to feed her people. While half of the world population borders on starvation, how is China, with little foreign assistance, able to nourish her masses?

Policies in agriculture
Not to detract from some of the achievements of the regime in the field of agriculture, it must be said that, considering the conditions in rural China at the 1949 takeover, it would have been difficult indeed not to have shown some growth in productivity during the early 1950s. In addition to persistent and recurring difficulties – floods and droughts, lack of farm implements, abuse of farm land, lack of fertilizer, excessive taxation and expensive credit – China had also just endured many years of war and civil strife and her rural economy was at a low ebb. Thus it was that, despite the confusion of these early years when the Communists were involved in land redistribution and the first stages of the creation of mutual-aid organizations, Peking was able to show an annual increase in agricultural production.

It is true that weather is the primary variable in Chinese agriculture; but for better or worse, organization and management have run a close second. To gain support of the peasants, the first step in rural reform undertaken by Peking was the redistribution of land – a political manœuvre that created as many problems as it solved. Not only were the most successful peasants penalized, but many of the land holdings, after redistribution, had become too small for practical farming. To help offset this handicap the regime introduced mutual aid teams. Since mutual help was common in many parts of China, it was not too diffi-cult to install first the seasonal or temporary and then the permanent mutual aid teams. This first step in formal cooperation involving the sharing of manpower, draught animals and agricultural tools was quite readily accepted by the peasants.

Before half of the Chinese peasant households were involved in the mutual aid programmes, the Communists started to experiment with agricultural producer cooperatives. The lower agricultural producer cooperatives further consolidated the small land holdings and increased controls over the rural population. The next step in the progression of

agrarian policy was to introduce higher agricultural producer cooperatives which were responsible for making the land holdings a part of
collective ownership rather than just cooperatively worked. By 1956
almost ninety per cent of the peasant households were part of the higher
agricultural producer cooperatives. It was also in this year that the idea
of private plots was promulgated, allowing each household to have a
small piece of land for its own use.

In the summer of 1958 the Communists introduced the people's
communes into rural China – the most drastic change yet imposed on
the peasants. The communes, which 'spontaneously' sprang up in the
rural areas, preceded the official proclamation incorporating producers'
cooperatives into the communes by some half a year. These new large
administrative bodies were to combine both political and economic
functions, thus furthering administrative and economic decentralization. Private property was virtually eliminated, including the private
plot of only two years' standing, and need rather than work determined
the distribution of food, goods and services. By September 1959 there
were 24,000 communes, subdivided into 500,000 brigades and over
three million production teams.

The problems and pressures created by the commune system and the
excesses and abuses of the Great Leap Forward shared the responsibility with unusually poor weather over most of China for the 'three
bitter years' that followed. The combination of these factors forced
the regime gradually to modify the commune system and to adjust
rural priorities. The Great Leap dream of rural industrialization was
abandoned and all national resources were mobilized for the task of
increasing food production. The size of the communes was reduced –
though they grew in number to 74,000 by 1964 – and at the same time
their role became rather vague. Most of the responsibilities were
returned to the small production team with its twenty to thirty families,
yet individuals once again enjoyed the personal incentives which had
been discontinued during the Great Leap. In rural areas this meant
the return of the private plot to the peasant household.

Although the Cultural Revolution was primarily an urban phenomenon, it had its inevitable effects in the countryside. The policy of self-
sufficiency in rural health, education, commerce, and other fields was
extended to food production. In furthering this policy the regime, seeking greater efficiency, elected to concentrate more of the planning and
production authority in a larger administrative unit – a return to the

K

philosophy prevalent during the establishment of the communes in 1958 – and the production brigades became the primary managing unit in rural China. At the same time that political yo-yo the private plot once again became a dilemma for Peking. The Cultural Revolution had as one of its basic objectives the elimination of 'revisionist material incentives', and yet, through practical experience, Peking had learned the disproportionate role that private plots play in the country's food production. Although steps were taken to confiscate them or reduce them in size, official statements persisted in assuring the sanctity of private plots and family pigs. At the time of writing the exact status of private plots is still uncertain. The numerous shifts in the broad policies inspired by political considerations did not really disrupt continuity in the programmes for increasing production of food.

China's efforts to enlarge the cultivated area have been mentioned in previous chapters. As with every other figure on China, estimates of arable land vary considerably. Not only have the Chinese themselves revised their figures many times, but Western estimates as well have differed by over a hundred per cent. Agreement, however, is almost unanimous with regard to two points: first, that China still has large areas of 'wastelands' which could be made fit for agriculture through human effort; and secondly, that any such effort to bring the un-cultivated areas into production would require tremendous capital investment in transportation, irrigation, chemical fertilizers, flood con-trol, drainage, afforestation of adjacent watersheds and other time-consuming enterprises. The horrendous problems involved in opening virgin lands in China's peripheral provinces were not fully appreciated until such a task was attempted in the 1950s. Now, although some effort aimed at increasing the cultivated acreage continues, the major emphasis of the regime has been, and will be, on increasing the productivity of land already under cultivation in the primary agricultural regions. Furthermore, the whole problem of land-management has been in-creasingly stressed in recent years. Even new industrial enterprises – particularly those now being established in rural areas – are urged to take special care not to occupy farmland in building factories, and instances are quoted where in the process of constructing plants on barren hillsides, additional land was actually reclaimed (by using fill) for agriculture.

It has already been mentioned that China's agricultural production depended directly on the frequency of floods and droughts which virtually every year affected large regions of the country. Consequently, to a very large extent the country's agricultural success depends on how well she manages her water resources. At least one-third of the country's cultivated land is irrigated. Since 1949 China's persistent efforts to harness and exploit rainfall, surface water and groundwater have resulted in a variety of successes and failures. For maximum efficiency there should be large-scale, uninterrupted and coordinated projects. The Communists did build a number of large-scale conservation works. They have also utilized literally hundreds of millions of man-years in draining marshes, terracing slopes, building irrigation canals and other related activities. However, all too often (and especially during the Great Leap) the mass earth work projects associated with water resources turned out to be poorly planned, poorly built, and completely and wastefully inadequate. On balance, however, the results have been beneficial and the priority for flood control and irrigation remains high.

The speed with which to mechanize agriculture, or for that matter whether to mechanize it at all, has been in dispute since the regime came to power. First of all, only a limited area in China is flat enough and large enough to permit the efficient utilization of tractors and combines. Secondly, there is the usual problem of priorities between heavy agricultural equipment and China's other civilian and military needs. Thirdly, the introduction of large mechanical devices would have the disadvantageous effect of replacing the already under-employed, abundant labour force. Fourthly, there is the problem related to the lack of skilled manpower (and spare parts) to operate and maintain heavy agricultural machinery. The arguments and complaints, as reported in the media, have not disrupted China's continued production and importation of tractors, combine harvesters, farm trucks and other units for mechanization of agriculture. Interrupted by the Great Leap, production picked up again in the mid 1960s. The use of agricultural machinery in areas most adaptable to mechanization has increased significantly, but China is still far from achieving the rather vague goal proclaimed in 1955 of 'complete mechanization' within twenty to twenty-five years.

Actually much of the emphasis has been on the less glamorous forms of 'mechanization' which, according to Chinese usage, includes everything from small mechanical equipment to improved farm implements, and to the use of rubber tyres on horse- or man-drawn vehicles. It is also closely related to 'electrification' of the countryside. Here, small electrically-operated pumps for irrigation and drainage have been extremely effective in increasing crop production. Now that many of the local industries have been moved into the rural areas and been given responsibility for the production of so much of the small tools and equipment in support of agriculture, the rate of mechanization and electrification is very likely to pick up.

As is true of all traditional agriculture, the Chinese farmer has always relied on organic fertilizers such as manure, straw, mud from streams and ponds, ashes and the like. The use of chemical fertilizer was insignificant prior to 1949. The Communists rapidly increased both the domestic production and importation (primarily from Western Europe and Japan) of chemical fertilizer; nevertheless, its use per unit of cultivated land has been very low. It was not until 1961, after the crop failures of the preceding several years, that chemical fertilizer got top priority in the scheme of the country's economic needs. In addition to the construction of small, medium and large plants producing both nitrogenous and phosphatic fertilizers, the Chinese have been importing large quantities of chemical fertilizers and even fully assembled fertilizer plants. Priority for the production of chemical fertilizer continues and, as in the case of mechanization, emphasis on local industry scattered throughout the provinces should markedly increase the number of small plants and the supply of fertilizer, while diminishing the problems of distribution. It must also be assumed that with greater availability, there will be a gradual improvement in the know-how – so important in the effective use of chemical fertilizer – and in the acceptance of this input, still so new to many Chinese peasants yet to be convinced the extra cost will pay off in increased yield. Despite these advances, the importance of natural fertilizer, which will continue to exceed chemical fertilizers for many years to come, should not be underestimated.

In addition to the progress made in the control of the basic agricultural inputs of land, water and fertilizer, the Communists have significantly increased all types of activities in agricultural research and development. The independent Chinese Academy of Agricultural Science was established in 1957 and its network of provincial and local research institutes, experimental stations and demonstration farms, was spread throughout most of the agricultural regions of the country. At least one agricultural college was set up in almost every province, coordinating many of their educational and experimental activities with the Academy. National policies and research combined to bring considerable progress in the control of insects and pests, in the development of new and more productive strains of seeds, close planting, double-cropping and so forth.

Finally, a few words about agricultural manpower without which all other inputs are for naught. It has already been pointed out that there was a gradual improvement in the 'quality' of the Chinese peasant. Through education and indoctrination he has become more aware and probably more efficient. Intentionally or not, the main benefits of the Cultural Revolution, which directed so much of its fury on the more advanced educational system and the people who were its products, may well have accrued to the rural population. With the increase in the number of graduates from secondary and even higher educational institutions in the rural areas and with the continued heavy investment in irrigation, rural electrification and mechanization, Peking is trying to create a new breed of scientific farmers, maintaining, as it did in 1970, that 'we must also arm the peasants with the latest scientific technology in chemistry, physics, soil science, entomology and microbiology'. The plan is, of course, over ambitious, but it should in the long run move Chinese agriculture in the right direction. It should also tend to break down the Chinese peasant's natural conservatism and resistance to change – a trait often decried in the Chinese press – and make him more favourably disposed toward the use of new grains, new fertilizers and new cultivation methods. Of late, the Chinese have indicated a growing awareness of the importance of effective planning and leadership in bringing about increases in agricultural production, stressing the need to plan, to calculate costs, and to allocate labour resources efficiently. Given the post-Cultural Revolution atmosphere it is quite possible that this time they will be more successful in accomplishing these goals.

The above run-down of agricultural advances in China may well seem too rosy, giving the impression that Peking has solved all its food problems. This conclusion, of course, would be incorrect. Furthermore, even some of the more thoughtful agricultural plans and policies suffered due to a lack of scientific know-how and from general mismanagement in implementation. For example, the early successful battle against grain-eating sparrows resulted in an increase of insects; there were instances of over-intensive use of fertilizer; the digging of thousands of wells accelerated the depletion of underground waters; overambitious deep-ploughing brought to the surface poorer soils that required more fertilizer and water. Thus the advances in agriculture should be viewed within the total context of the developments and policies of the People's Republic – primarily as long-term trends and practices.

Agricultural production

Because the last officially reported figure on grain production usually accepted without serious reservations and adjustments is for 1957, the guessing game as to China's grain output is almost as frantic as the one on population, the estimates differing by a much larger percentage than do the population figures. This is not really surprising. Whereas population estimates are, to some extent, controlled by physiological limits on fertility and mortality, in the case of agricultural production there is disagreement as to the area under cultivation; the area planted to food crops; the yield per acre of the various crops; the amount of fertilizer available and applied and the effect of fertilizer on the yield; acreage that is double-cropped; the extent and effect of mechanization; the area that is under irrigation; the annual effects of weather and other natural phenomena; the extent of use of improved seed and pesticides; the amount held back from human consumption; and more. There is only one hope: that the errors implicit in these various calculations will tend to cancel each other out. The magnitude of the problem is clear from the fact that those making grain production estimates tend to lean on population estimates as support for their figures. This may be flattering to demographers, but is not too reliable since the range of population projections is so great that there is always a figure to support any estimate of food production.

Within the context of a study of population, it should be adequate to present just the general trends in agricultural production without a debate of all the pros and cons of the various estimates. The last acceptable figure reported by Peking was 185 million metric tons of grain for 1957 – a culmination of a series of increasing figures that started in 1949. There was another increase in production in 1958, but nowhere near the exaggerated Great Leap figure of 250 million tons – amended by the Chinese themselves the following year. This was followed by the already mentioned failures in Chinese agriculture, with grain production dropping to about 150 to 160 million tons in 1960 and then gradually increasing again (with a few minor set-backs) throughout the remainder of the 1960s. Most estimates seem to place the 1970 grain production in China at between 220 and 230 million tons.

Since 1961 Chinese production has been supplemented by the importation of between four and five million tons of wheat per year, primarily from Canada and Australia; this despite an increasing trend in domestic production and a continuous increase in the export of agricultural commodities (indeed, in 1966 such exports exceeded agricultural imports). There are a number of reasons offered for the continuing importation of wheat. The most important consideration must surely be that on the world market the price of rice, which is exported, is nearly double the price of wheat, which is imported.

Having considered the total amount of grain available in China, the next natural step is to divide that figure by the country's population and, on the basis of the per capita grain production (and even calorie intake), conclude that the population has grown more rapidly than the output of grain and that the Chinese must at best be on a subsistence diet, and at worst close to mass starvation. This simplistic approach disregards other evidence which would contradict the conclusion. Certainly private visitors and foreign officials assure us that there are no visible indications of any serious food shortages either in the cities or in the countryside. Furthermore, although in a country where the people have traditionally relied on grain crops for their basic food supply and grain production is rightly used as the primary index for survival, perhaps not enough attention has been paid to other sources of food and to the individual's ingenuity when it comes to providing for the family's daily food requirements.

China's livestock population is of course closely related to her grain production, and to certain state policies which in some years have resulted in excessive slaughter of animals. Nevertheless, since the food-deficit years of the early 1960s, the livestock population has been steadily increasing. Large animals in China are used primarily for draught purposes, but with the establishment of breeding centres and veterinary stations in many parts of the country, the number of hogs, sheep and other small domestic animals has increased. The Chinese have also been reporting substantial increases in the production of fish and other marine products. To do this they have enlarged their fishing fleet and motorized their junks and trawlers, making it possible for them to go out further to sea and to stay away longer periods of time. Fishing communes are also devoting an ever-increasing proportion of their time to the breeding of kelp, mussels, clams, oysters, abalone and other

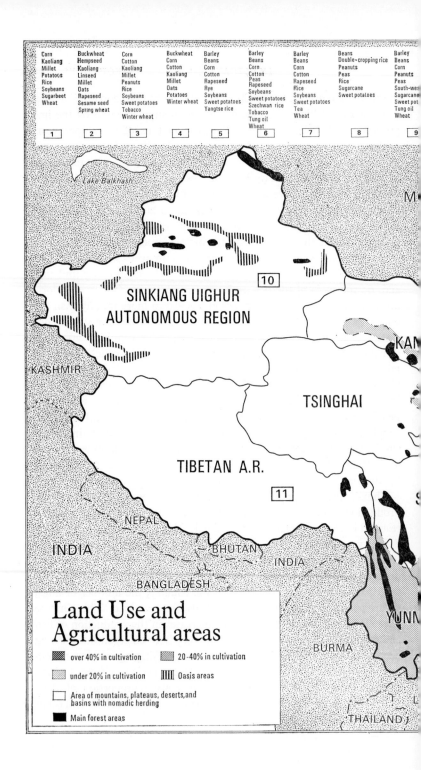

Corn	Buckwheat	Corn	Buckwheat	Barley		Barley	Barley	Beans	Barley
Kaoliang	Hempseed	Cotton	Corn	Beans		Beans	Beans	Double-cropping rice	Beans
Millet	Kaoliang	Kaoliang	Cotton	Corn		Corn	Corn	Peanuts	Corn
Potatoes	Linseed	Millet	Kaoliang	Cotton		Cotton	Cotton	Peas	Peanuts
Rice	Millet	Peanuts	Millet	Rapeseed		Peas	Rapeseed	Rice	Peas
Soybeans	Oats	Rice	Oats	Rye		Rapeseed	Rice	Sugarcane	South-wes
Sugarbeet	Rapeseed	Soybeans	Potatoes	Soybeans		Soybeans	Soybeans	Sweet potatoes	Sugarcane
Wheat	Sesame seed	Sweet potatoes	Winter wheat	Sweet potatoes		Szechwan rice	Sweet potatoes		Sweet pot
	Spring wheat	Tobacco		Yangtse rice		Tobacco	Tea		Tung oil
		Winter wheat				Tung oil	Wheat		Wheat
						Wheat			
1	**2**	**3**	**4**	**5**	**6**	**7**	**8**		**9**

Lake Balkhash

M

SINKIANG UIGHUR
AUTONOMOUS REGION

10

KASHMIR

KAN

TSINGHAI

TIBETAN A.R.

11

NEPAL

INDIA

BHUTAN

INDIA

BANGLADESH

YUNN

Land Use and
Agricultural areas

- ▨ over 40% in cultivation
- ▨ 20-40% in cultivation
- ▦ under 20% in cultivation
- ⦀ Oasis areas
- ☐ Area of mountains, plateaus, deserts, and basins with nomadic herding
- ■ Main forest areas

BURMA

THAILAND

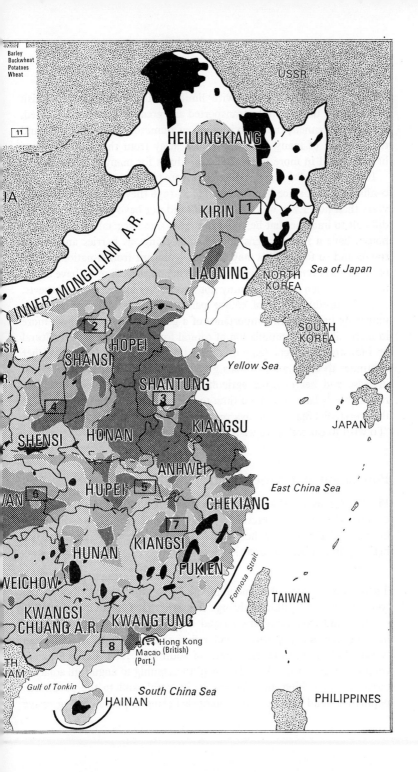

Barley
Buckwheat
Potatoes
Wheat

11

USSR

HEILUNGKIANG

KIRIN 1

INNER-MONGOLIAN A.R.

LIAONING

NORTH KOREA

Sea of Japan

SOUTH KOREA

2

HOPEI

SHANSI

SHANTUNG 3

Yellow Sea

4

SHENSI

HONAN

KIANGSU

JAPAN

ANHWEI

6

HUPEI 5

CHEKIANG

East China Sea

7

KIANGSI

HUNAN

FUKIEN

WEICHOW

Formosa Strait

TAIWAN

KWANGSI CHUANG A.R.

KWANGTUNG

8

Hong Kong (British)
Macao (Port.)

TH
AM

Gulf of Tonkin

South China Sea

HAINAN

PHILIPPINES

marine products. Although with limited refrigeration facilities, fish products are unlikely to be transported any great distance unless salted, smoked or canned, the establishment of numerous fish hatcheries and the stocking of many lakes and ponds away from the coastal regions have resulted in more fish and fish products for many more people.

It is true that the very productive private plots have on occasion been confiscated, but since their innovation in 1956 they have survived more years than not. Even when the peasant did not have access to one, it is difficult to imagine that he could not grow some vegetables close to his house, have a few chickens, gather such things as berries and mush-rooms and so forth. This may seem insignificant from a national point of view, and even naïve. But the man living on the soil must have access to edibles which would certainly not appear on national balance sheets.

Grain production is of course paramount, but unless there is an unusually bad crop the importance of a good harvest may weigh more in increasing the accumulation of capital for investment in agricultural or industrial projects than in preventing starvation. If the weather continues to be an ally, China's gradually declining rate of population increase and her growing agricultural productivity should remain in reasonable balance for some time to come. And if the worst comes to the worst, Peking can always resurrect the 1965 newspaper headline: 'To wish to eat well is to wish to be a bourgeois capitalist.'

Population and power politics

Finally, let us consider China's population within the international context. Does China represent a threat to her neighbours or the world because of the size of her population and the precarious balance between it and her resources?

Forces for expansion

There is a substantial element in the West which subscribes to the 'yellow peril' or 'spillover' theory; this says that China's population is so large and expanding at so rapid a rate, and her resources are so limited, that the population will either spill over into the Siberian 'vacant lot' or into the 'rice bowl' of south-east Asia. References are commonplace to the 'blanket of men' threatening to engulf all adjacent territories, 'crushing any obstacle in its path', and to the precarious population-food balance which 'compels Peking to pursue an aggressive policy'. It is not my aim here to deny the existing tensions on China's borders. Certainly Peking's uninhibited vocal belligerency is not always sufficiently tempered by restraint of action to permit a relaxation of vigilance by any of China's neighbours. I would suggest, however, that neither population pressures nor food shortages are the motivating factors in China's border policies and that the periodic crises are generated rather by political considerations.

China's overall population density of approximately 185 persons per square mile is lower than that of many countries of Europe and Asia, yet none of them is considered a threat simply by virtue of their population. It is the uneven distribution of China's population (see chapter 4), which gives rise to the theory of overpopulation. Traditional rural unemployment and underemployment are additional relevant factors. With these considerations it is apparent that the shortage is not in *land* per se, but in *arable land* which is severely limited by topography and climate.

The preceding sections of this chapter should make it evident that Peking is actively pursuing a variety of policies to cope with both labour utilization and food production. If properly implemented, these policies should meet with reasonable success. The Chinese appear to be quite serious when they say that a nation with one-quarter of the world's population must solve the problem of increasing food needs within its own borders.

But even if there is no major pressure to cross international boundaries, is there anything vital to China's needs on the other side of her borders? China is rimmed by eleven nations, but those who fear her potential population pressure vis-à-vis the surrounding countries usually refer to the Soviet Union (and sometimes to Mongolia) as the target for space, and south-east Asia as the target for food. Let us examine these premises.

Siberia has about half the land area of the Soviet Union but only ten per cent of the population for an average density of some five persons per square mile. Actually, Siberia has hundreds of thousands of square miles of virtually unpopulated territory with only three per cent of its area cultivated and most of the population concentrated in a swath along the trans-Siberian railway. There is no significant food surplus produced in this region. Most of Siberia is in the permafrost region and her severe climate limits the growing season. Although some expansion of the cultivated land is possible, it would require considerable capital investment and effort.

Farther west and south are the arid lands of Soviet central Asia. Although a little more densely populated than Siberia, only ten per cent of these 1·2 million square miles are cultivated and much of that land is planted to cotton. Most of the grain is hundreds of miles from the Chinese border in the virgin land development area of Kazakhstan.

The Soviet areas adjoining China may rightly be called a 'vacant lot', but the same may be said of thousands of square miles on the Chinese side of the border which are just as sparsely populated. As a matter of fact, the unmarked boundary between China and what is now Soviet central Asia has been crossed and recrossed by the nomadic peoples inhabiting those lands for many centuries, neither knowing nor caring who claimed the territory on which their animals grazed.

According to Peking, it is the vast areas in the north and north-west of China that hold the key to many of the country's aspirations. They represent the country's frontier and contain vast natural resources of great importance to the country's economic plans. China is not only generously endowed with most of the basic mineral resources; she also has large reserves of coal, large amounts of oil have been found and waterpower resources are immense. In some cases the extraction costs may be high and some of these resources may not be conveniently located, but demonstrated progress in these activities indicates that China need not go outside her borders in search of natural resources.

Economic growth to date was naturally accompanied by an in-migration of people from the central provinces – in-migration that should continue as the transportation system and the economic potential of these areas are further developed. On the average China's border provinces receive fewer than a million migrants a year, a figure too insignificant in terms of the densely populated central provinces to be a reflection of any policy designed to relieve population pressure. Potentially, at least, the outer circle of Chinese provinces and autonomous regions should be able to support several times their present population without undue pressures on the Soviet border.

It is, in fact, somewhat surprising that the Russians themselves often express the fear of Chinese hordes crossing their border. One writer even suggested that Khrushchev's appeal to Russian women to have three or four children was in anticipation of the need to defend Siberia from the overflowing Chinese masses. Actually, population pressure was not a factor in the Sino-Soviet tensions of the early 1960s nor in the actual military confrontation on the Amur in the late 1960s. To view the relationship in its proper perspective it is necessary to remember that it was the decade of the 1950s – the short period of cooperation – that was unique in the history of the two powers. There is a traditional, deep-rooted animosity between the countries and their peoples harking back hundreds of years. This historical mistrust is the result of constant territorial quarrels along much of their 4,500-mile border. Yet, despite the fact that some of the border areas are considered potentially rich in mineral resources, given the will on the part of the two adversaries, the border problems need not be difficult to negotiate and adjust. The regions under dispute on either side of the boundary are sparsely populated and, with a few insignificant exceptions, the Russians have taken no territory inhabited or effectively ruled by the Chinese, which suggests that the real roots of hostility between China and the Soviet Union are not related to the population–land ratio, but must be found elsewhere; specifically in arguments over ideology, in national pride, and in racial differences.

Now what about south-east Asia? Is it really a 'rice bowl' that could solve China's food shortages? Most of the countries of south-east Asia have, in fact, been rice surplus areas and in that sense the area qualifies as a 'rice bowl'. But even prior to the extension of the Indo-China conflict the total rice exports of the area would have represented only about a two-per-cent increase in China's grain output. This certainly should negate any thesis that Peking covets south-east Asia as an area with a potential for contributing to the feeding of China's hungry millions. Besides, the practical considerations in any forceful occupation of south-east Asia would be overwhelming. Considering the historical fear of the Chinese in that part of Asia, a sizeable military force would be needed to occupy those countries and undoubtedly there would be continual unrest and rebellion which would hamper food production. Also, China's image in other underdeveloped countries (so important to Peking) would be badly damaged. It is difficult to imagine a more inefficient way of solving her agricultural problems than to undertake invasion to get something which could be obtained far more efficiently by trade – a course she has been pursuing.

The overseas Chinese
Another fear commonly expressed in relation to China's population refers to the large number of people of Chinese ancestry living dispersed around the world, and especially in the countries of south-east Asia.

According to Claude Buss, an historian and former American Foreign Service officer: 'The overseas Chinese will have no more influence on the future of China than Boston policemen will have on the future of Ireland.' Undoubtedly true; however the important question is not their influence on China, but rather their influence, if any, on the future of the country in which they reside. Or to put it more pointedly: does a significant proportion of the overseas Chinese (particularly in south-east Asia) maintain a mental or a sentimental allegiance to the Peking government, and in that sense constitute a built-in fifth column for a militant Communist China? A preponderance of evidence suggests a negative answer.

Table 16: Geographic distribution of overseas Chinese

place of residence	June 1965[1]	June 1969[2]	per cent increase
Asia	16,975,424	17,573,352	3·5
Americas	449,774	551,570	22·6
Europe	34,148	62,092	81·8
Oceania	50,992	63,688	24·9
Africa	47,429	50,424	6·3
Total	17,557,767	18,301,126	4·2

[1] *China Yearbook 1965–6* (Taiwan), p. 266.
[2] *China Yearbook 1969–70* (Taiwan), p. 394.
Note: Includes individuals with dual citizenship. Because the individual figures reflect migration, there are significant differences in the annual rates of increase. The average annual increase of only one per cent in the number of overseas Chinese is surprising, especially since their number includes at least a few thousand migrants from mainland China and Taiwan every year. Among the factors that may be responsible are the inaccuracy of the statistics, assimilation and a significant excess of males in the reproductive ages. The Communist Census of 1953 reported only 11,743,320 overseas Chinese.

There are now almost twenty million Chinese who live outside the borders of the People's Republic and Taiwan – ninety-six per cent of them in Asia (see table 16). Most were originally from the provinces of Kwangtung and Fukien. Some emigrated as recently as 1949; others are descendants of migrants who departed their homeland centuries ago. Most Chinese parents have successfully instilled a sense of cultural heritage in their children; nevertheless, over the course of several generations large numbers of Chinese settlers have been completely assimilated within the countries of south-east Asia. The more recent migrants remain Chinese and maintain certain cultural bonds with China, while identifying their economic futures with their adopted homes. In general the overseas Chinese have achieved their enviable economic positions through hard work and by keeping out of local politics. It was only after 1949 that they found themselves in a political tug-of-war between Peking and Taipei, for both capitals were anxious to attract their sympathy and support – support not necessarily essential but certainly a useful bonus to either one.

It is impossible to draw conclusions which would encompass any group as large and as diverse as the overseas Chinese. There are not only individual differences of opinion and aspiration, but also differences emanating from the policies and conditions of the countries in which they live. Despite this caveat, the majority of expert opinion about overseas Chinese agrees on two basic points: first, that although Peking competes for the support of the overseas Chinese, for the most part it carefully avoids using them in pursuit of political goals; and secondly, that no matter what their individual leanings might be, most overseas Chinese prefer to be left alone to concentrate on their personal economic aims.

Peking realizes that to support indigenous nationalism through the use of overseas Chinese on the one hand and pursue a policy of peaceful coexistence on the other would immediately result in unfavourable repercussions. Chou En-lai clearly expressed this view in his 1956 speech in Burma: 'We do not promote the organization of communist or other democratic parties among the overseas Chinese . . . this would invite misunderstanding in the countries of residence.' He further called on the overseas Chinese 'to obey the laws, and respect the customs, habits and religious beliefs of the countries of residence'. This does not mean, of course, that China would not if the opportunity were right support indigenous revolutionary activities, or that some Chinese cadres might not be used in leading such a movement; but Chou's statement does seem to reflect Peking's general policy of not using the masses of overseas Chinese as a subversive force. The Chinese know that any revolutionary activity by the overseas Chinese would result in real or suspected connection with Peking and would therefore prejudice the whole revolutionary movement.

Probably the most convincing verification of the above conclusions comes from some of the attacks in Red Guard publications during the Cultural Revolution on Liao Ch'eng-chih, Chairman of the Overseas Chinese Affairs Commission at the time and effective head of the commission since 1949. He was accused of dissolving all political and educational organizations among overseas Chinese that were supporting (or were supported by) the Peking regime, merely so that the suspicion of the local government would not be aroused. As a matter of fact, Liao is quoted as saying that overseas Chinese should not make revolution and that if they do they will not succeed. The most damning accusation of Liao by the Red Guards was that his goal was to allow the overseas Chinese to become independent of China and thus let the Overseas Chinese Affairs Commission to work itself out of existence. Extreme as the Red Guard accusations were, they were usually based on fact and there is no reason to believe that Liao was not expressing or implementing the official policies of the Chinese government.

During the Cultural Revolution the receptiveness of the overseas Chinese to Peking's propaganda was at a low ebb, for they too reacted with shock and distaste to some of the extreme activities of those years. Nevertheless, the admission of the People's Republic of China into the United Nations probably erased many bad memories from the minds of those who tended to be sympathetic towards Peking, and it may even have shaken the confidence and hope of those overseas Chinese who have 'an attachment' to the Nationalist Government. The sympathy of many of the latter was not necessarily translated into support for Taiwan – an island that did not hold any sentimental values – and was therefore quite ambiguous and vulnerable.

In general, however, the preference of most of the overseas Chinese is to continue to be just that – overseas Chinese. Most of them undoubtedly feel a certain pride in the accomplishments of the People's Republic and, after a century of humiliation, her status as a world power. Yet for the most part, they are deeply involved in capitalist endeavours and are neither willing to serve as tools of the Peking regime, nor ready to give up economic security for ideological struggle. As for Peking, it has said little with regard to the overseas Chinese since 1968 and apparently, despite Red Guard criticism, the considerations that restrained China in the past will continue to shape her policies and objectives in the immediate future.

Conclusion

China's reputation as an expansionist nation should not be associated with her population; it results primarily from an overemphasis on her continuous and acrimonious tirades against imperialists and revisionists and on Mao's often-quoted dictum that 'political power grows out of the barrel of a gun', and ignores the caution she has exhibited in committing her military forces. References to China as an aggressive, expansionist nation first of all, and quite naturally, point to instances when there was either a serious threat or an actual use of armed force by Communist China. Most interpretations of these 'disputes', however, deny Chinese action as a reflection of a policy directed at territorial expansion. Many of the goals of the People's Republic of China, particularly as they relate to the Asian continent, coincide with those that would be held by any strong Chinese government, whether Communist or not. China is genuinely concerned about encirclement by hostile nations and is anxious to eliminate all Western influence (the 'white peril') in her part of the world so that she can concentrate on establishing political and economic hegemony. The Chinese are sincere in their belief that revolutionary movements in Asia, Africa and Latin America will eventually be victorious – the notion that the 'countryside' will eventually engulf the 'cities'. They recognize, however, that this is a long-term objective and stress that success can come about only through the efforts of the peoples of the countries involved.

Despite China's tendency to balance objective against risk, there is no guarantee that, given certain conditions which in the opinion of her leadership would pose a serious threat to her security (or even to her very sensitive pride), China might not initiate military activities which would defy normal logic. This would not be an action to pursue expansionist goals, but rather a reaction to external conditions which she might interpret or misinterpret as provocative and threatening.

All this is not meant to imply that China is not interested in expanding her influence and ideology among the emerging nations of Asia, Africa and Latin America. She is. In the process she hopes not only to eliminate or at least greatly curtail Western influence, but also to replace the Soviet Union in the leadership of the world communist movement. But the reverses in Chinese diplomacy suffered in 1965 and 1966 have probably proved to Peking that the country is not yet sufficiently powerful to achieve its ambitious goal, particularly with

L

regard to geographically distant nations. China may have also realized that her very specialized version of militant communism is not necessarily an easy commodity to sell. It must be stressed, however, that China's overall objectives as they pertain to world communism have not changed: when she feels that the national and international situation is once again propitious, she is likely to speed up her disruptive activities in the developing countries of the world.

These suppositions notwithstanding, there is still no evidence that the Chinese leadership attempts to seek territorial expansion for any economic motives. China's militancy may be a reflection of any number of national objectives: it may be a desire to spread international communism; it may be a determination to restore China to its past grandeur; it may simply be a means of eliciting greater sacrifice from the people of China. But this militancy is not the result of pressures generated by masses of Chinese people in search of *Lebensraum*. The People's Republic of China is well aware that there is no immediate solution in the adjacent countries to her population/food dilemma and is making every effort to resolve it internally. And finally, this may be solace to those who look into the distant centuries and see the inevitability of the Chinese race overrunning the world: the proportion of Chinese to the total population of our globe is, slowly but surely, decreasing.

Appendix· Sources of data for the People's Republic

Most writers on China are prone to lament the data gaps and point to the analytical limitations which stem from inadequate information – a condition that certainly pervades this study. The lack of factual information on contemporary China is undeniable, but it is easy to project this complaint into a number of erroneous conclusions. The reader might choose to believe that if the country were not controlled by the Communists or if there were more free access to visit the People's Republic, we would have at our disposal all the necessary data to research, analyse and, therefore, to understand China. Let us consider this assumption.

It is important to realize that, despite such periods as the Cultural Revolution when publication of most sources ceased, it is still possible to turn to the 1950s and even the mid 1960s, when the Chinese Communist presses were running off quantities of published materials of every conceivable variety. Just because much of it is propaganda (most blatant in the foreign news area) and presented in unique Chinese Communist jargon, we should not arbitrarily dismiss it as worthless. Newspapers and magazines are not published just to deceive the unsuspecting reader in a foreign government agency or a university. When data are published they are intended as a communication to the people of China and as guidelines to the cadres in the performance of their duties. When conditions become particularly unfavourable – as, for example, in the early 1960s – Peking simply ceases publishing meaningful materials and concentrates its efforts on political pep talks. The flow of sources out of China naturally fluctuates with the ups and downs in Peking's own publication policies, but a very substantial proportion of significant information does find its way out of the country. What then is the problem and why the contradiction?

The basic explanation is that there is a tendency to expect too much; because China is a nuclear power we assume she has a modern information base. This is unrealistic. When one thinks of China as an under-developed country – which she still is – and compares the available information with that for some of the other less developed nations of Asia, Africa and Latin America, expectations become more realistic. Although there are rich historical records, detailed descriptions of people and culture, essays on religion and the arts, and literary works that cover all facets of life in ancient China, there is little reliable information for the first half of this century which could serve as a starting point for assessing many of the social, economic and political developments since 1949. There is an inclination to forget that social sciences in China have never progressed beyond the infancy stage. There has always been a lack of adequate social science information in China and it is therefore unreasonable to expect that Peking could improve the situation substantially in just a few turbulent decades.

Our unreasonable expectations are particularly apparent in those fields requiring hard facts and figures. We suspect that, because China is a closed society and because the Communists are, in fact, obsessed with secrecy, all the answers we seek are there – merely hidden behind security walls and combination locks. The existence of secrets is manifest, but it is posed here that the answers are not and that in many instances the data problem is just as great for the Chinese as it is for persons looking at China from the outside. When a Chinese scholar or bureaucrat wishes to study certain aspects of the Chinese economy, consider questions relating to population and manpower, or look into any subject demanding quantitative interpretation and analysis, he is likely to face many of the same data gaps which hinder a Western analyst. It is very likely the former has information not available to the outsider; it is most unlikely he has all the necessary statistics and back-up materials.

Since the contention here is that the Chinese themselves lack much of the data we in the West seek, a complete lifting of travel restrictions would not solve all the problems. This is not to deny the importance of what can be learned from first-hand observation – the insights to be gained concerning various policies and their implementation, and the mood and temperament of the nation and its people. But nothing reported either by private visitors or embassy personnel justifies the conclusion that access to China would lay open vast sources of data.

And yet the contradiction remains: although the incomprehensibility of the whys and wherefores of many of the developments in China is frustrating, it is entirely wrong to say (as so many do) that 'we know nothing about Communist China'. Proof is in the scores of excellent and in many cases definitive studies on the People's Republic of China written by a large number of qualified specialists. The inevitable disagreements apparent in their work and the inability authoritatively to quantify some of the conclusions do not detract from the scholarship and great understanding of the country, the government, the people and the problems of China. Furthermore, Chinese experience in social sciences has been so limited that what a Western scholar may lack in terms of data vis-à-vis his Chinese counterpart, he can compensate for in many instances by his extensive experience in theory and in methods of handling inadequate and gap-ridden data, and by his greater overall sophistication. The unpredictability of China's leadership and the difficulty of rationalizing many of its policies do pose special problems of forecasting, but even in our 'open' societies with the omnipotent computerized data banks, how many pundits are willing or able to foretell what will happen in our own countries; and of those who do make predictions of the future, how many are correct?

Volume and content of data
In China it is not merely a matter of the state controlling the mass media, for the mass media are actually a part of the nation's political structure. News of all current developments is disseminated via the newspapers, the radio and a few specialized journals and most of it is supplied by the New China News Agency (NCNA), which is under the usual dual control of the party and the state. Changes in Peking's policies – the extent to which 'politics are in command' – are therefore immediately reflected in the volume and content of what is made available to the Chinese people.

   In addition to the *People's Daily* (Jen-min Jih-pao), which has been and continues to be the most influential and most widely circulated paper, there were five other newspapers of national significance prior to the Cultural Revolution: *Kuang-ming Daily* (cultural and educational news), *Ta Kung Pao* (economic and financial news), *China Youth Daily* (the organ of the Communist Youth League), the *Daily Worker* (the organ of the All-China Federation of Trade Unions) and the *Liberation Army Daily*. Each province also published a newspaper, as did the large cities, many of the smaller urban areas, and even some rural communes. That there were probably no more than three newspaper copies for every hundred people even during the better years is no indication of the impact of this media. Because of the low literacy rate in China, Mao has always relied more on the spoken word – the radio – to communicate to the masses. That is why most of the important articles in the press are always read on the local radio stations. In addition, newspaper reading (study and discussion) groups were established throughout the countryside and it was the individual's patriotic duty to listen to the cadres read and explain the prescribed texts.

   The Cultural Revolution ended the publication of most newspapers and hundreds of popular magazines, literary journals, publications of special organizations and academic journals. Thus, the most significant articles have appeared only in the *People's Daily*, *Liberation Army Daily*, and *Red Flag*. The radio stations, however, continued to operate throughout the Cultural Revolution and reliance on radio broadcast (no matter how insignificant the substance) had to increase accordingly.

There are several periods which can be distinguished in terms of volume and validity of data emanating from the⁅People's Republic. Although these periods are particularly discernible when reviewing the statistical data, a definite correlation exists between the accuracy and volume of statistics and the validity of accompanying text.

The first phase covers 1949–52 and may be described as one of retrenchment and consolidation. The new regime was more concerned with organizing its systems of administration and control than with the collection and publication of meaningful information about conditions in the country. Much of the data used undoubtedly was inherited from the old regime, while results of some of the surveys conducted by the successors were in their own words 'neither adequate in coverage nor accurate'.

The State Statistical Bureau was not established until the latter part of 1952, and from 1953 to 1957 – the period of the First Five-Year Plan – a gradual improvement was noted in both the quality and quantity of statistics and other materials which made somewhat more fruitful the task of following developments. Without question the best information on Communist China was available during the three years between 1955 and 1957. Through the concentrated efforts of the State Statistical Bureau, the statistical system began to produce data which were, for the most part, more reasonable and acceptable. This was a period when ministers delivered periodic reports, when ministries published specialized journals, and when the lengthy speeches to the People's Congresses occasionally held information of some substance, not otherwise available. In addition this period includes 1957, the year when the hundred flowers bloomed and the hundred schools of thought contended. In inviting the people to criticize the regime, Mao Tse-tung opened Pandora's box; he was stunned (and the world, too, was surprised) by the critical outburst of public opinion which, during the short six weeks, exposed so many of the country's intimate problems.

The effect of the Great Leap Forward in 1958 on the validity of data published in China is notorious. The movement which was to transform Communist China overnight into a modern industrial nation by exhorting maximum effort from all segments of the population collapsed with predictable force, dragging down with it the whole statistical system. Statistics became the 'weapon of the class struggle' and, by decree, not a 'mere display of objective facts'. This deterioration in statistics resulted in the contamination of all media of information, so that almost everything published during 1958 and the first part of 1959 had to be scrutinized carefully, and usually adjusted, for statistical and political bias.

In 1959 the regime tried to recoup the errors of the previous year. In the area of statistics, the government admitted overestimating production goals, initiated a campaign to improve the accuracy of figures, and at the same time once again centralized the control of statistics under the more responsible vertical authority of the State Statistical Bureau. These efforts to improve statistical reporting were not very successful, however. The Great Leap disruption was too great to reverse rapidly, especially since the non-statistical coverage in Communist publications continued to express the Great Leap attitude of exaggeration and swagger.

The economic crisis that followed the Great Leap drastically affected the information media of Communist China. The number of titles of published books and journals decreased tremendously, perhaps from some 30,000 in the late 1950s to about 5,000 in 1961. As reported by the Chinese, the reduction was due to a shortage of paper and the general need to concentrate the limited resources in areas of higher priority. However, very typically the regime also was unwilling to report anything which would reveal the intensity of the internal problems China was trying to overcome during these post-Leap years. As conditions began to improve, the number of monographic titles increased and publication of suspended periodicals was resumed. Although the level of information never reverted to the retrospectively daring period of the First Five-Year Plan, the easier atmosphere from 1963 to 1965 did result in temporary relaxation in the content of published materials – only to see another reversal with the gradual approach of Mao's Cultural Revolution.

Because the Cultural Revolution was directed primarily at the urban professional class of the society, it was quite natural that it would have drastic effects on the nation's press. Furthermore, it would not be an exaggeration to say that virtually all available presses and newsprint were utilized in printing literally hundreds of millions of copies of Mao's writings. Most other publications were suspended and book-publishing houses were closed; in their place appeared revolutionary 'big-character posters' and tabloid newspapers issued by the various factions of Red Guards. Thousands of these posters plastered on the walls of China's cities, plus the Red Guard publications, provided those watching the internal power struggles and the ups and downs of individual leaders with voluminous (if often unreliable) materials for speculation. For other China-watchers, with only radio broadcasts allowing some minimal insight into conditions in the country, it was a period of almost complete informational blackout.

As the Cultural Revolution gradually ran its course, China's few publications began to supplement the protracted texts devoted to the adoration of Mao with occasional, substantive information – bits and pieces that could only seem encouraging. The flow of information continued to improve gradually in 1970, for although the number of titles published remained extremely small, more stable conditions in the country apparently permitted coverage in greater detail of some economic, social and political developments. It is reasonable to assume that eventually many of the publications suspended in 1966 and 1967 will reappear, albeit under new management and probably sporting a new format.

Availability of sources
In a sense, the question of what and how much the Chinese publish is strictly academic. From the viewpoint of those studying the Chinese scene from outside, of greater relevance is how much of the published material becomes available to them. Unfortunately it is extremely difficult to estimate the proportion of Chinese-language materials published in China which finds its way beyond the borders. During the middle and late 1950s, it could have been as high as twenty to twenty-five per cent for monographs and forty to fifty per cent for periodical titles. In the autumn of 1959 the Communists placed an unofficial ban on the export of scores of scholarly journals and other publications – many of which ceased publication during the ensuing few years anyway. By 1962 the ban was relaxed to permit a gradual increase in the flow of Communist publications. Cutbacks in publication during the Cultural Revolution simplified China's controls over printed materials leaving the country; Peking had only to be concerned about smuggled Red Guard publications and copied wall posters.

The proportion of sources which leave the country is not necessarily a very meaningful index either, since included in China's publication statistics are thousands of children's books, song books, modern literature, picture stories, and other publications of only very specialized interest. Besides, many of these books and pamphlets are duplicates, independently published in different provinces. A large number of technical books are translations from Western languages and are available in the original abroad. Some of the listed titles represent only new editions of old publications. Many significant articles appearing in newspaper and periodical literature are reprinted in several sources. Thus, in determining the proportion of Communist sources available abroad, it would be more realistic to subtract from the base figure the number of less consequential publications in order to compare the 'actual take' against the 'desirable take'. If such an adjustment were possible, it would result in a much different and, of course, more favourable data picture.

What about the channels through which source materials from China are acquired – when these materials are available? Two very direct methods often come as a surprise: one is to subscribe to periodicals which are mailed directly from Peking; the other is to visit or write to one of a number of Western bookstores which are outlets for Communist Chinese publications. It is true that the selections available through these channels are rather limited. Much of the material in English (usually translations) published by the Foreign Languages Press in Peking has a propaganda content that is anything but subtle. Most publications can be described as politically cumbersome (international relations, international communism, political documents, etc.) or insignificant (sports, hobbies, literature, arts, etc.). Not everything obtainable through the Foreign Languages Press publications can be ignored, however, some of the monographs represent important basic sources, while an experienced reader often can find valuable information by wading through the propaganda journals.

The bulk of the Chinese language publications which find their way out of China, however, continue to be purchased by universities and by government purchasing agents from various independent book dealers, most of which are located in Hong Kong. In addition to the large over-the-counter business, there is a thriving black market in Communist publications and it is generally understood that, for an appropriate price, booksellers will make a (not always successful) effort to procure almost any publication originating in the People's Republic. They may be limited editions of books, specialized periodicals, or simply local newspapers which are banned from export by the regime, but which contain important and often unique information.

Other important sources of Chinese publications that in many instances were not available through any other channel have been exchange agreements between the Peking Library and the Institute of Scientific and Technical Information of the Chinese Academy of Sciences and some of the Chinese libraries in leading American universities. For the most part such agreements were limited to professional journals and scientific and technical material which the Chinese were particularly anxious to obtain, and at the height of these exchanges several hundred thousand published items were exchanged every year (1955-7). The nature of the 'take' was often quite specialized and, in that sense, more valuable.

The Japanese government and a few universities sponsor considerable research on Communist China, but presumably most of the publications available in these institutions are also purchased on the open market, either in one of the Tokyo book stores which specialize in Chinese materials or in Hong Kong. It is quite possible that such left-wing organizations as the Chinese Research Institute receive materials that are not otherwise available. Unfortunately, they are not anxious to share their sources. Very little Japanese research on China has been translated into English; furthermore, on the basis of the small sample available, the work is not over impressive. Scholars and other Japanese visitors to the People's Republic occasionally bring back sources not generally obtainable, but as a rule the selections in Hong Kong are richer. A possible exception is in the field of commerce and industry. Japanese businessmen, anxious to expand their trade with China, sometimes come by otherwise unavailable data on industrial facilities and production.

One would normally expect Taiwan to be a gold mine for information on the People's Republic. After all, who should have better channels for procurement of Communist publications or for other information as to the developments inside China? The problem, however, is one of security: it is difficult to evaluate the holdings on Taiwan since so much of the work is conducted in classified government agencies such as the Bureau of Intelligence of the Ministry of National Defense, the Bureau of Investigation, and similar organizations. Although during the last few years studies published on Taiwan have become somewhat more available and even more objective than had previously been the case, whether to protect 'covert' sources or for other reasons, the government has not been overly eager to lend assistance to foreign students of Communist China, and many of the original sources and final reports continue to be classified and unavailable. There are, however, a number of non-official institutes where students can do research on developments in the People's Republic.

Just what kind of research on China takes place behind the Kremlin's closed doors, what kind of sources are available to the Russian intelligence specialist, is of course impossible to say. If we are to accept the word of some Soviet China specialists, the USSR did not take full advantage of her presence in China during the 1950s in terms of collecting all available published materials. On the contrary, because they were fraternal nations it was presumed unnecessary to exert special efforts along this line – any data supposedly would be available on request. As for the period since 1960 after the Russians pulled out of China, it is unlikely that their procurement channels have been superior to those in Hong Kong. Despite the envy of some Soviet scholars when viewing specialized American libraries with their extensive holdings of Communist Chinese publications, the major libraries in the Soviet Union (such as Moscow and Leningrad) also contain extensive collections which undoubtedly include many sources unavailable in the West. It is probably true, however, that the Russians have no magic sources or formulas that would provide them with unusual insights as to the forces and the developments in the People's Republic of China.

Many other countries study contemporary China. Such centres as exist in England, France, Germany, some of the countries of East Europe, Australia, India and elsewhere, collect and maintain Chinese materials on a larger or smaller scale, but it can be said with considerable confidence that the resources on Communist China available in the United States both in academic centres and the unclassified government sector are superior to any collection outside China herself.

Translations; other basic sources in English

Although many of the researchers concentrating their efforts on contemporary China have mastered the very difficult Chinese language, many more rely on a variety of English-language translations of official Communist publications – most of them supported by the United States Federal Government. Surprisingly, even many of the native Chinese often prefer to save time by using the conveniently organized translated materials in their research, only occasionally relying on the vernacular sources in a supplementary way or to check possible ambiguities in translation. Thus, it is ironic but true that because of these translations and because such a large proportion of finished research on China is published in English, the English language has become almost indispensable for research on China.

The United States Joint Publications Research Service (JPRS) was established in 1957 to provide US Government agencies with necessary translations of materials primarily from Communist countries. The JPRS publishes several series of translations covering the full range of subjects from politics and economics to physical sciences and technology. How much is translated depends to a large extent on the volume of publication in China. Thus, in the middle 1950s when the Chinese presses were working at near capacity, the proportion translated by JPRS and other translation services was naturally much lower. During the early 1960s and especially since 1966, virtually all important articles in the available sources were provided in translation. In addition, now that so little is being published in China, many translations are made of earlier sources which had been unavailable or bypassed because of low priority. At present the JPRS publishes two serial reports on Communist China: *Translations on Communist China* and *Scientific Abstracts*, also an irregularly published series on social sciences.

The United States Consulate in Hong Kong supports a translation unit which regularly produces three important publications that for many years have served as one of the principal sources for academic research on the Chinese mainland. *The Survey of the China Mainland Press,* previously a daily, is now issued weekly and contains in full or in summary form all the important newspaper articles. As the title indicates, *Selections from China Mainland Magazines* (formerly *Extracts from China Mainland Magazines*) carries full translations from selected articles from nontechnical periodicals, and is now issued monthly (formerly a weekly). *Current Background* is published on an ad hoc basis, each issue concentrating on one subject or topic and presenting full translations or extracts from a variety of sources. A *Quarterly Index* of all material issued during the three-month period is also published.

Another basic source of materials in English is the *Daily Report* (Communist China), published by the Foreign Broadcast Information Service (FBIS). It offers news developments from Communist China which have been monitored from their radio broadcasts, the New China News Agency transmissions, newspapers, and periodicals published within the preceding forty-eight to seventy-two hours. Each item is clearly marked as a complete rendering of the text, an excerpt, or a summary. Somewhat similar service is provided by the British Broadcasting Corporation (BBC), which also monitors Chinese broadcasts. Since September 1970 public access to all three of the US-sponsored translation series has been merged, making them available through subscription to the National Technical Information Service (NTIS) of the US Department of Commerce.

The Union Research Institute in Hong Kong also engages in translating various Chinese materials into English. Since 1955 it has been publishing twice weekly the *Union Research Service* – a topical survey of China's press and provincial radio broadcasts. The Union Research Institute collects and processes Chinese Communist journals, newspapers, magazines, books, pamphlets, handbills and wall posters. Extensive clipping files are broken down according to subject and are available to scholars, students and journalists. On the basis of these resources the Institute has also been producing books and monographs that are based almost entirely on well-documented Communist sources.

Finally, there are three secondary sources which fall into the 'almost indispensable' category for the study of contemporary China. Published in London since 1960, *The China Quarterly* is the single most important professional journal devoted to the study of Communist China. It contains articles by most of the foremost specialists covering all conceivable areas of study. *Current Scene* has been published in Hong Kong by the United States Information Agency since 1959. Until recently it was a bi-weekly publication, with each issue containing a fairly detailed article either by a guest contributor or by the editors. Now it is a monthly, with a leading article and a few shorter items in each issue. The *China News Analysis*, a weekly newsletter since 1953, continues to be published by Father L. LaDany in Hong Kong. Each issue usually covers a single topic, relying almost entirely on Chinese Communist sources for the data and using generous quotations from them.

Bibliography

As an employee of the Library of Congress I have access to an endless stream of sources which contribute to my musings and attitudes. To list them all would be a formidable if not an impossible task. Instead, I shall limit this bibliography to those sources specifically relevant to the question of China's population and manpower. Even within this framework the list is selective, for despite the paucity of reported population data on China, judged by the volume of publications, it is obvious the subject has intrigued many people over the years. Furthermore, those writing on the population of the People's Republic of China would probably be the first to admit that, because of the data problem, the same figures and even the same interpretations are of necessity often repeated. For the same reason there is a tendency to write general articles incorporating all available information, rather than to concentrate on specific issues and problems requiring more detailed data. This is why the bibliography is subdivided only in terms of years of publication and does not include a detailed subject breakdown.

With the exception of some articles in French and one in Russian, only sources in English are included. Much of the material appeared prior to 1950 in publications not readily available in most libraries – many of them in English-language professional journals and newspapers published in China during the first half of this century. Only a sampling of these writings is included. Of the materials published since the establishment of the People's Republic of China, with the exception of a few illustrative English-language publications from Peking, all the raw data are omitted. It is assumed that anyone interested in doing research in depth on the population of present-day China would have other ways of getting at this raw data in the original Chinese articles or their translations. Many additional writings, both valuable and pertinent to the subjects covered in this monograph, are contained in such basic sources as *The China Quarterly, China News Analysis, Current Scene,* and the *Far Eastern Economic Review.*

Published before 1950

JOHN W. ALEXANDER, 'The Prewar Population of China: Distribution and Density', *Annals of the Association of American Geographers*, XXXVIII, No. 1 (March 1948), pp. 1–5.

M. C. BALFOUR, et al., *Public Health and Demography in the Far East: Report of a Survey Trip, 13 September–13 December 1948* (New York: Rockefeller Foundation, 1950).

MINER S. BATES, *The Nanking Population: Employment, Earnings and Expenditures* (Shanghai: Mercury Press, 1939).

G. W. BARCLAY, 'China's Population Problem: A Closer View', *Pacific Affairs*, XXIII, No. 2 (June 1950), pp. 185–92.

JOHN LOSSING BUCK, et al., *Land Utilization in China*, 3 vols. (Chicago: University of Chicago Press, 1937).

CHANG CHIH-I, 'China's Population Problem – A Chinese View', *Pacific Affairs*, XXII, No. 4 (December 1949), pp. 339–56.

CHAO CH'ENG-HSIN, 'Recent Population Changes in China', *Yenching Journal of Social Studies*, I, No. 1 (Peiping: June 1938), pp. 1–48.

CH'EN CH'ANG-HENG, 'Some Phases of China's Population Problem', *International Statistical Institute Bulletin*, XXV, Pt. 2 (1930), pp. 18–54.

CH'EN TA, 'Factors of Urban Growth in China', *Proceedings of International Statistical Conference*, III, Pt. B (September 1947), pp. 733–43.

— *Population in Modern China* (Chicago: University of Chicago Press, 1946).

CHEN TS'AI-CHANG and CH'IAO CH'I-MING, 'Birth and Death Rates in Kiangyin Registration Area', *Economic Facts*, No. 1 (Nanking: September 1936), pp. 66–71.

WARREN H CH'EN, 'An Estimate of the Population of China in 1929', *International Statistical Institute Bulletin*, XXV, Pt. 2 (1930), pp. 55–87.

— 'Recent Population Statistics', *China Critic*, II, No. 16 (Shanghai: 18 April 1929), pp. 313–15.

CHIANG CHIH-ANG, 'Using the Pao as the Primary Sampling Unit. Some Notes and Reflections on the Possibilities of a Census of China by Sampling', *Population Studies*, II, No. 4 (London: March 1949), pp. 444–53.

CH'IAO CH'I-MING, 'Rural Population and Vital Statistics for Selected Areas of China, 1929–1931', *Chinese Economic Journal*, XIV, No. 3 (Shanghai: March 1934), pp. 304–36; XIV, No. 4 (Shanghai: April 1934), pp. 391–425.

CH'IAO CH'I-MING, and CH'EN TS'AI-CHANG, 'Factors Affecting the Birth Rate in China', *Economic Facts*, No. 4 (Nanking: February 1937), pp. 181–8.

176 EVERY FIFTH CHILD

CH'IAO CH'I-MING, WARREN S. THOMPSON, and D. T. CHEN, *An Experiment in the Registration of Vital Statistics in China* (Oxford, Ohio: Scripps Foundation, 1938).

'China in Statistics', *Chinese Social and Political Science Review*, XIV, No. 4 (Peiping: October 1930), pp. 445–70.

'Current Estimates of the Size and Distribution of China's Population', *Population Index*, XIV, No. 1 (January 1948), pp. 3–20.

FEI HSIAO-TUNG, 'Agricultural Labor in a Yunnan Village', *Nankai Social and Economic Quarterly*, XII, No. 1–2 (Tientsin: June 1941), pp. 146–68.

— *Peasant Life in China. A Field Study of Country Life in the Yangtze Valley*. (New York: E. P. Dutton, 1939).

H. D. FONG, 'Industrialization and Labor in Hopeh', *Chinese Social and Political Science Review*, XV, No. 1 (Peiping: April 1931), pp. 1–28.

HARRY PAXTON HOWARD, 'China's Population and the Present Census', *China Critic*, II, No. 24 (Shanghai: 13 June 1929), pp. 471–4.

— 'Chinese Population Fig_res', *China Critic*, II, No. 23 (Shanghai: 6 June 1929), pp. 449–52.

— 'Population Pressure and the Growth of Famine in China', *Chinese Economic Journal*, IV, No. 2 (Shanghai: March 1929), pp. 248–62.

— 'Present Population of China', *China Critic*, II, No. 25 (Shanghai: 20 June 1929), pp. 491–4.

L. S. HSU, 'Some Aspects of the Chinese Population Problem', *Chinese Social and Political Science Review*, XIV, No. 3 (Peiping: July 1930), pp. 281–312.

A. J. JAFFE, 'A Review of the Censuses and Demographic Statistics of China', *Population Studies*, I, No. 3 (London: December 1947), pp. 308–37.

— 'Notes on the Rate of Growth of the Chinese Population', *Human Biology*, XIX, No. 1 (February 1947), pp. 1–11.

FENTON KEYES, 'Urbanism and Population Distribution in China', *American Journal of Sociology*, LVI, No. 6 (May 1951), pp. 519–27.

H. O. KUNG, 'The Growth of Population in Six Large Chinese Cities', *Chinese Economic Journal*, XX, No. 3 (Shanghai: March 1937), pp. 301–4.

H. D. LAMSON, 'Differential Reproduction in China', *Quarterly Review of Biology*, X, No. 3 (September 1935), pp. 308–21.

— 'Population Studies: Size of the Chinese Family in Relation to Occupation, Age, and Education', *Chinese Economic Journal*, XI, No. 6 (Shanghai: December 1932), pp. 478–96.

OLGA LANG, *Chinese Family and Society* (New Haven: Yale University Press, 1946).

FRANKLIN C. H. LEE, 'An Analysis of Chinese Rural Population', *Chinese Social and Political Science Review*, XIX, No. 1 (Peiping: March 1935), pp. 22–44.

D. K. LIEU, 'A Brief Account of Statistical Work in China', *International Statistical Institute Bulletin*, XXV, Pt. 2 (1930), pp. 88–121.

— 'Earlier Statistical Work in China', *China Critic*, III, No. 45 (Shanghai: 6 November 1930), pp. 1061–5.

— 'Industrial Development and Population Problem', *China Critic*, III, No. 10, (Shanghai: 6 March 1930), pp. 226–8.

— 'The 1912 Census of China', *International Statistical Institute Bulletin*, XXVI (1931), pp. 85–109.

— 'Statistical Work under the National Government', *China Critic*, III, No. 47 (Shanghai: 20 November 1930), pp. 1136–40.

LIU NANMING-I, *Contribution a l'Etude de la Population Chinoise*. Ph. D. dissertation, Faculty of Letters, University of Paris (Geneva: Imprimerie et Editions Union, 1935).

'Manchuria as a Demographic Frontier', *Population Index*, XI, No. 4 (October 1945), pp. 260–74.

WILLIAM W. ROCKHILL, 'An Inquiry into the Population of China', in *Annual Report of the Board of Regents of the Smithsonian Institution for the Year Ending June 30, 1904* (Washington: US Government Printing Office, 1905), pp. 659–76.

HARRY B. SEIFERT, 'Life Tables for Chinese Farmers', *Milbank Memorial Fund Quarterly*, XIII, No. 3 (July 1935), pp. 223–36.

WARREN S. THOMPSON, *Plenty of People* (New York: Ronald Press, 1948).

— *Population and Peace in the Pacific* (Chicago: University of Chicago Press, 1946).

BORIS P. TORGASHEFF, 'Town Population in China', *China Critic*, III, No. 14 (Shanghai: 3 April 1930), pp. 317–22.

WALTER F. WILLCOX, 'The Population of China and its Modern Increase', in his *Studies in American Demography* (Ithaca, New York: Cornell University Press, 1940), pp. 511–40.

GERALD F. WINFIELD, 'Population Control', in his *China: the Land and the People* (New York: William Sloane Associates, Inc., 1948), pp. 334–59.

WONG WEN-HAO, *The Distribution of Population and Land Utilization in China* (Shanghai: China Institute of Pacific Relations, 1933).

WU CHING-CH'AO, 'Chinese Immigration in the Pacific Area', *Chinese Social and Political Science Review*, XII, No. 4 (Peiping: October 1928), pp. 543–60.

FRANK S. C. YEN, 'Rural Population in China', *Sociology and Social Research*, XXII, No. 4 (April–May 1938), pp. 421–7.

YUAN I-CHIN, 'Life Tables for a Southern Chinese Family from 1365 to 1849', *Human Biology*, III, No. 2 (May 1931), pp. 157–79.

Published since 1949

JOHN S. AIRD, *Estimates and Projections of the Population of Mainland China: 1953–1986.* US Bureau of the Census, International Population Reports, Series P–91, No. 17 (August 1968).

— 'Estimating China's Population', *Annals of the American Academy of Political and Social Science*, CCCLXIX (January 1967), pp. 61–72.

— 'Population Growth', *Economic Trends in Communist China*, edited by A. Eckstein, *et al.* (Chicago: Aldine Publishing Co., 1968), pp. 183–327.

— 'Population Growth and Distribution in Mainland China', *An Economic Profile of Mainland China*, US Congress, Joint Economic Committee (New York: Frederick A. Praeger, 1968), pp. 341–401. (Praeger Special Studies in International Economics and Development.)

— 'Population Growth: Evidence and Interpretation', *China Quarterly*, No. 7 (July–September 1961), pp. 44–56.

— 'Population Policy in Mainland China', *Population Studies*, XVI, No. 1 (July 1962), pp. 38–57.

— *The Size, Composition, and Growth of the Population of Mainland China.* US Bureau of the Census, International Population Statistics Reports, Series P–90, No. 15. (July 1961).

EDWIN G. BEAL, JR., 'The 1940 Census of Manchuria', *Far Eastern Quarterly*, IV, No. 3 (May 1945), pp. 243–62.

PETER BENDER, 'Divorce Chinese Style', *Atlas*, IX, No. 6 (June 1965), pp. 348–52.

CLAUDE A. BUSS, 'Chinese in Southeast Asia', *Understanding Modern China*, edited by J. M. Kitagawa (Chicago: Quadrangle Books, 1969), pp. 184–201.

The Census Results', *China News Analysis*, No. 61 (Hong Kong: 26 November 1954).

SRIPATI CHANDRASEKHAR, *China's Population: Census and Vital Statistics.* 2d ed., revised and enlarged (Hong Kong: Hong Kong University Press, 1960).

—'China's Population Problems: A Report', *Population Review*, III, No. 2 (Madras: July 1959), pp. 3–38.

— 'Marx, Malthus and Mao: China's Population Explosion', *Current Scene* (Hong Kong: 28 February 1967), pp. 1–14.

— 'Population Planning in China', *Population Review*, II, No. 2 (Madras: July 1958), pp. 49–58.

CHANG SEN-DOU, 'The Historical Trend of Chinese Urbanization,'

Annals of the Association of American Geographers, LIII, No. 2 (June 1963), pp. 109–43.

CHAO KANG, 'Industrialization and Urban Housing in Communist China', *Journal of Asian Studies*, XXV, No. 3 (May 1966), pp. 381–96.

CHEN LIN, 'A Study of the Chinese Mainland Population', *Issues and Studies*, No. 2 (Taipei: November 1968), pp. 17–25.

CHEN PI-CHAO, 'China's Birth Control Action Programme, 1956–1964', *Population Studies*, XXIV, No. 1 (London: July 1970), pp. 141–58.

CHEN TA, 'New China's Population Census of 1953 and its Relations to National Reconstruction and Demographic Research', *Bulletin de l'Institut International de Statistique*, XXXVI, No. 2 (1958), pp. 255–71.

'China's Birth Control Campaign', *Far Eastern Economic Review* (Hong Kong: 4 April 1957), pp. 421–2.

CHOU WEI-PIN, 'Our First Scientific Census', *People's China*, No. 7 (Peking: 1 April 1955), pp. 17–23.

CHOW PEI-YUAN, 'Population, Production, and Birth Control', *Bulletin of the Atomic Scientists*, XIV, No. 2 (October 1958), pp. 325, 333.

CHUNG SU, 'Facts about China's Population', *Peking Review*, I, No. 18 (Peking: 1 July, 1958), pp. 9–10.

COLIN CLARK, 'L'Accroissement de la Population de la Chine', *Population*, XIX, No. 3 (June–July 1964), pp. 559–68.

— 'La Population de la Chine depuis 1915', *Population*, XXI, No. 6 (Paris: November–December 1966), pp. 1191–200.

ROBERT C. COOK, 'China's Achilles Heel: Explosive Population Growth', *Population Bulletin*, XII, No. 8 (December 1956), pp. 129–45.

GEORGE B. CRESSEY, *Land of the 500 Million* (New York: McGraw-Hill Co., 1955).

'The 1953 Census of China', *Far Eastern Quarterly*, XIV, No. 3 (May 1955), pp. 387–8.

JOHN DE FRANCIS, 'National and Minority Policies', *Annals of the American Academy of Political and Social Science*, CCXXVII (September 1951), pp. 146–55.

THOMAS E. DOW, 'The Population of China', *Current History*, LV, No. 325 (September 1968), pp. 141–6.

'Drawing the Line: Family Reform', *China News Analysis*, No. 571 (Hong Kong: 9 July 1965).

JEAN DRESCH, 'Population et Ressources de la Chine Nouvelle', *Annales de Géographie*, LXIV, No. 343 (Paris: 1955), pp. 171–201.

JUNE DREYER, 'China's Minority Nationalities in the Cultural Revolution', *China Quarterly*, No. 35 (London: July–September 1968), pp. 96–109.

JOHN D. DURAND, 'Generalized Demographic Models and Projections of the Population of China', *Asian Survey*, I, No. 4 (June 1961), pp. 29–34.

— 'The Population Statistics of China, AD 2–1953', *Population Studies*, XIII, No. 3 (London: March 1960), pp. 209–56.

JOHN PHILIP EMERSON, 'Chinese Communist Party Views on Labor Utilization Before and After 1958', *Current Scene* (Hong Kong: 20 April 1962), pp. 1–10.

— 'Employment in Mainland China: Problems and Prospects', *An Economic Profile of Mainland China*, US Congress, Joint Economic Committee (New York: Frederick A. Praeger, 1968), pp. 403–69. (Praeger Special Studies in International Economics and Development.)

— 'Manpower Absorption in the Non-Agricultural Branches of the Economy of Communist China, 1953–58', *China Quarterly*, No. 7 (London: July–September 1961), pp. 69–84.

— *Nonagricultural Employment in Mainland China: 1949–1958*. US Bureau of the Census, International Population Statistics Reports, Series P–90, No. 21 (March 1965).

— *Sex, Age, and Level of Skill of the Nonagricultural Labor Force of Mainland China*, US Bureau of the Census (Washington: 1965).

GILBERT ETIENNE, 'Quelques Données Récentes sur la Population de la Chine', *Population*, XVII, No. 3 (Paris: July–September 1962), pp. 459–64.

ROBERT MICHAEL FIELD, 'A Note on the Population of Communist China', *China Quarterly*, No. 38 (London: April–June 1969), pp. 158–63.

STEPHEN FITZGERALD, 'Overseas Chinese Affairs and the Cultural Revolution', *China Quarterly* No. 40 (London: October–December 1969), pp. 103–26.

MICHAEL FREEBERNE, 'Birth Control in China', *Population Studies*, XVIII, No. 1 (London: July 1964), pp. 5–16.

— 'Changing Population Characteristics in Tibet, 1959 to 1965', *Population Studies*, XIX, No. 3 (London: March 1966), pp. 317–20.

— 'Demographic and Economic Changes in the Sinkiang Uighur Autonomous Region', *Population Studies*, XX, No. 1 (London: July 1966), pp. 103–24.

'The Spectre of Malthus: Birth Control in Communist China', *Current Scene* (Hong Kong: 15 August 1963), pp. 1–14.

HAN SUYIN, 'Family Planning in China', *Japan Quarterly* (Tokyo: October–December 1970).

TOSHIO HAYASE, 'Overseas Chinese in South-east Asia', *Oriental Economist*, XXXIII, No. 660 (Tokyo: October 1965), pp. 580–4.

HAROLD C. HINTON, 'Colonization as an Instrument of Chinese Communist Policy', *Far Eastern Economic Review* (Hong Kong: 24 October 1957), pp. 513–22.

— 'The National Minorities in China', *Far Eastern Economic Review* (Hong Kong: 15 September 1955), pp. 321–5.

HO, PING-TI, *Studies in the Population of China, 1368–1953* (Cambridge, Massachusetts: Harvard University Press, 1959).

CHARLES HOFFMANN, 'Industrial Work-Incentives in Communist China', *Current Scene* (Hong Kong: 1 May 1963), pp. 1–13.

HOU CHI-MING, 'Manpower, Employment, and Unemployment', *Economic Trends in Communist China*, edited by A. Eckstein, et al. (Chicago: Aldine Publishing Co., 1968), pp. 329–96.

JOYCE K. KALLGREN, 'Social Welfare and China's Industrial Workers', *Chinese Communist Politics in Action*, edited by A. Doak Barnett (Seattle: University of Washington Press, 1969), pp. 540–73.

ALINE KAN, 'The Marriage Institution in Present-Day China', *China Mainland Review*, I, No. 3 (Hong Kong: December 1965), pp. I–II.

E. STUART KIRBY, 'China's Population Problem', *Far Eastern Economic Review* (Hong Kong: 24 April 1958), pp. 513–7.

— 'The New Approach to Population Policy in Asia', *Far Eastern Economic Review* (Hong Kong: 13 October 1955), pp. 449–52.

— 'Peiping's Growing Dilemma: Population', *Problems of Communism*, VII, No. 2 (March–April 1958), pp. 36–41.

SIDNEY KLEIN, 'A Note on Statistical Techniques in Communist China', *American Statistician*, XIII, No. 3 (June 1959), pp. 18–21.

S. KROTEVICH, 'Vsekitayskaya perepis naseleniya 1953 g (All-China population census of 1953)', *Vestnik Statistiki*, No. 5 (Moscow: September–October 1955), pp. 31–50.

AMRIT LAL, 'Early Fertility-Management Concepts in China', *Hawaii Medical Journal*, XXVI, No. 2 (November–December 1966), pp. 110–14.

— 'Fertility Management and Concern with Over-Population in Mainland China', *Eugenics Quarterly*, XI, No. 3 (September 1964), pp. 170–4.

LI CHO-MIN, *The Statistical System of Communist China* (Berkeley: University of California Press, 1962).

LING NAI-JUI, 'Population Problems of China: A Sceptical View', *Contemporary China*, edited by E. Kirby (Hong Kong: Hong Kong University Press, 1956), pp. 37–43.

M. G. D. MALMQUIST, 'The Population Problem of China', *Australian Outlook*, XIII, No. 2 (Sydney: June 1959), pp. 124–8.

'New Theory of Population for China', *Far Eastern Economic Review* (Hong Kong: 22 August 1957), pp. 225–6.

ERNEST NI, *Distribution of the Urban and Rural Population of Mainland China: 1953 and 1958*. US Bureau of the Census, International Population Reports, Series P–95, No. 56 (October 1960).

ETSUZO ONOYE, 'Regional Distribution of Urban Population in China', *Development Economies* (Tokyo: March 1970), pp. 93–127.

LEO A. ORLEANS, 'Birth Control: Reversal or Postponement?', *China Quarterly*, No. 3 (London: July–September 1960), pp. 59–70.

— 'China's Population: Reflections and Speculations', *Contemporary China*, edited by Ruth Adams (New York: Pantheon Books, 1966), pp. 239–52.

— 'Evidence from Chinese Medical Journals on Current Population Policy', *China Quarterly*, No. 40 (London: October–December 1969), pp. 137–46.

— 'A New Birth Control Campaign?', *China Quarterly*, No. 12 (London: October–December 1962), pp. 207–10.

— 'The 1953 Chinese Census in Perspective', *Journal of Asian Studies*, XVI, No. 4 (August 1957), pp. 565–73.

— 'The Population of Communist China', *Population: The Vital Revolution*, edited by R. Freedman (New York: Anchor Books, 1964), pp. 227–39.

— 'Population Redistribution in Communist China', *Population Trends in Eastern Europe, the USSR, and Mainland China*, Proceedings of a Round Table at the 36th Annual Conference of the Milbank Memorial Fund, 4–5 November 1959 (New York: Milbank Memorial Fund, 1960), pp. 141–50.

— 'Population Statistics: An Illusion', *China Quarterly*, No. 21 (London: January–March 1965), pp. 168–78.

— 'Problems of Manpower Absorption in Rural China', *China Quarterly*, No. 7 (London: July–September 1961), pp. 57–68.

— *Professional Manpower and Education in Communist China* (Washington, National Science Foundation, 1961).

— 'Propheteering: the Population of Communist China', *Current Scene* (Hong Kong: 15 December 1969), pp. 13–19.

— 'The Recent Growth of China's Urban Population', *Geographical Review*, XLIX, No. 1 (January 1959), pp. 43–57.

PAN CHIA-LIN, 'An Estimate of the Long-Term Crude Birth Rate of the Agricultural Population of China', *Demography*, III, No. 1 (1966), pp. 204–8.

Population and Family Planning in the People's Republic of China, the Victor-Bostrom Fund and the Population Crisis Committee, edited by P. T. Piotrow (Washington: Spring 1971).

'Planned Birth Rate', *China News Analysis*, No. 172 (Hong Kong: 15 March 1957).

ROLAND PRESSAT, 'La Population de la Chine et son Economie', *Population*, XIII, No. 4 (Paris: October–December 1958), pp. 569–90.

— 'La Population de la Chine: Structure et Evolution Récente', *Population*, XVI, No. 4 (Paris: October–December 1961), pp. 649–64.

— 'The Present and Future Demographic Situation in China', *Proceedings of the World Population Conference, 1965*, United Nations, Department of Economic and Social Affairs, Vol. II (New York: United Nations, 1967), pp. 29–33.

EARL H. PRITCHARD, 'Thoughts on the Historical Development of the Population of China', *Journal of Asian Studies*, XXIII, No. 1 (November 1963), pp. 3–20.

VICTOR W. PURCELL, *The Chinese in Southeast Asia* (London: Oxford University Press, 1965).

'Red China's New Population Policy', *Oriental Economist*, XXVI, No. 571 (Tokyo: May 1958), pp. 245–7.

ALFRED SAUVY, 'La Population de la Chine. Nouvelles Données et Nouvelle Politique', *Population*, XII, No. 4 (Paris: October–December 1957), pp. 695–706.

— 'La Recensement de la Chine', *Population*, XI, No. 4 (Paris: October 1956), pp. 725–36.

HENRY G. SCHWARZ, 'Chinese Migration to North-West China and Inner Mongolia, 1949–1959', *China Quarterly*, No. 16 (London: October–December 1963), pp. 62–74.

— *Chinese Policies Towards Minorities; An Essay and Documents*. Western Washington State College, Program in East Asian Studies, Occasional Paper No. 2. (Bellingham: Western Washington State College, 1971).

THEODORE SHABAD, 'Counting 600 Million Chinese', *Far Eastern Survey*, XXV, No. 4 (April 1956), pp. 58–62.

— 'The Population of China's Cities', *Geographical Review*, XLIX, No. 1 (January 1959), pp. 32–42.

EDGAR SNOW, 'Population Care and Control', *The New Republic*, (1 May 1971), pp. 20–3.

J. E. SPENCER, 'Agriculture and Population in Relation to Economic Planning', *Annals of the American Academy of Political and Social Science*, No. 321 (January 1959), pp. 62–70.

CHARLES SNYDER, 'Malthus versus Marx', *Far Eastern Economic Review* (Hong Kong: 26 December 1970), pp. 28–32.

IRENE B. TAEUBER, 'China's Population: Enigma of the Past, Riddle of the Future', *Antioch Review*, XVII, No. 1 (Spring 1957), pp. 7–18.

— 'Policies, Programs, and the Decline of Birth Rates: China and the Chinese Populations of East Asia', *Population Dynamics: International Action and Training Programs*, Proceedings of the International Conference on Population, May 1964, edited by M. Muramatsu and P. A. Harper (Baltimore: Johns Hopkins Press, 1965), pp. 99–104.

— 'Population Policies in Communist China', *Population Index*, XXII, No. 4 (October 1956), pp. 261–74.

IRENE B. TAEUBER and PAN CHIA-LIN, 'The Expansion of the Chinese North and West', *Population Index*, XVIII, No. 2 (April 1952), pp. 85–101.

— and WANG NAI-CHI, 'Population Reports in the Ch'ing Dynasty' *Journal of Asian Studies*, XIX, No. 4 (August 1960), pp. 403–16.

— — 'Questions on Population Growth in China', *Population Trends in Eastern Europe, the USSR, and Mainland China*, Proceedings of a Round Table at the 36th Annual Conference of the Milbank Memorial Fund, 4–5 November 1959 (New York: Milbank Memorial Fund, 1960), pp. 263–302.

S. K. TAI, *1953 Population Census of China* (Calcutta: Indian Statistical Institute, 1956).

WARREN S. THOMPSON, *Population and Progress in the Far East*, (Chicago: University of Chicago Press, 1959).

H. YUAN TIEN, 'Birth Control in Mainland China: Ideology and Politics', *Milbank Memorial Fund Quarterly*, XLI, No. 3 (July 1963), pp. 269–90.

— 'The Demographic Significance of Organized Population Transfers in Communist China', *Demography*, I, No. 1 (1964), pp. 220–6.

— 'Induced Abortion and Population Control in Mainland China', *Marriage and Family Living*, XXV, No. 1 (February 1963), pp. 35–43.

— 'Population Control: Recent Developments in Mainland China', *Asian Survey*, II, No. 3 (July 1962), pp. 12–16.

— 'Sterilization, Oral Contraception, and Population Control in China', *Population Studies*, XVIII, No. 3 (London: March 1965), pp. 215–35.

T. R. TREGEAR, 'Population Problems of China: An Optimistic View, *Contemporary China*, edited by E. S. Kirby (Hong Kong: Hong Kong University Press, 1956), pp. 32–6.

GLENN T. TREWARTHA, 'Chinese Cities: Numbers and Distribution', *Annals of the Association of American Geographers*, XLI, No. 4 (December 1951), pp. 331–47.

— 'Chinese Cities: Origins and Functions', *Annals of the Association of American Geographers*, XLII, No. 1 (March 1952), pp. 69–93.

— 'Newsmaps of China's Population', *Geographical Review*, LXVII, No. 2 (April 1957), pp. 234–9.

LEON TRIVIERE, 'Birth Control in China', *Contemporary China*, II, edited by E. S. Kirby (Hong Kong: Hong Kong University Press, 1956–63), pp. 94–9.

TSUNG YUN, 'China's National Minorities', *People's China*, No. 11 (Peking: 1954), pp. 17–23.

MORRIS B. ULLMAN, *Cities of Mainland China: 1953 and 1958*, US Bureau of the Census, International Population Reports, Series P–95, No. 59 (August 1961).

UNITED NATIONS (Department of Economic and Social Affairs), *Future Population Estimates by Sex and Age. Manual III: Methods for Population Projections by Sex and Age*, Population Studies No. 25, (New York: 1956).

— *Future Population Estimates by Sex and Age. Report IV: The Population of Asia and the Far East, 1950–1980*, Population Studies No. 31 (New York: 1959).

US BUREAU OF THE CENSUS, *An Estimated Distribution of the Population of Mainland China, by Age and Sex: June 30, 1953*, International Population Reports, Series P–91, No. 3 (June 1956).

— *Mainland China, 1949–1960*, Bibliography of Social Science Periodicals and Monographs, Series P–92, No. 3 (September 1961).

— *The Population of Communist China: 1953*, International Population Reports, Series P–90, No. 6 (4 March 1955).

— *The Population and Manpower of China: An Annotated Bibliography*, International Population Reports, Series P–90, No. 8 (June 1958).

KENNETH WALKER, 'Ideology and Economic Discussion in China: Ma Yin-Ch'u on Development Strategy and his Critics', *Economic Development and Cultural Change*, XI, No. 2, Part 1 (January 1963), pp. 113–33.

WANG SHU-TANG, *China – Land of Many Nationalities* (Peking: 1955).

W. F. WERTHEIM, 'Recent Trends in China's Population Policy', *Science & Society*, XXX, No. 2 (Spring 1966), pp. 129–35.

DICK WILSON, 'Counting the Heads', *Far Eastern Economic Review* (Hong Kong: 6 January 1966), pp. 22–3.

WALLER WYNNE, JR., *The Population of Manchuria*, US Bureau of the Census, International Population Statistics Reports, Series P–90, No. 7 (April 1958).

C. K. YANG, *The Chinese Family in the Communist Revolution* (Cambridge Massachusetts Institute of Technology, 1954).

Index

underemployment, 128
underpopulation, 35
unemployment, 128
United Nations, 13; Population
  Division, 56; and Peking's mem-
  bership, 160
US Bureau of the Census, 56
urban areas, number of, by size of
  place (table), 60; with over
  500,000 inhabitants, 61; inland,
  growth of, 83
urban communes, 65
urban labour force, 121–4
urban migration, 63–9; and 'blind
  infiltration', 63, 128
urban population, 57–72; early
  settlements, 57; 1953 census, 59;
  definition, 59–61, 72; percentages
  1949–56 (table), 62; during the
  Great Leap Forward, 65; of
  Shanghai, 64, 66; of Peking,
  66; during the Cultural Revolu-

tion, 67; trends in the 1950s,
  64, 121; trends in the 1960s, 67;
  future trends, 69; geographic
  distribution (table), 71; during
  the First Five-Year Plan, 83;
  after the Great Leap Forward,
  130, 134
urban–rural distribution, 1953 census, 17

water resources, 147
women, 1953 census, 17; exclusion
  from registers, 28
workers and employees, and urban
  growth, 66; number, 1949–58,
  121

youth, attitudes of, 45; deportation
  from cities, 45; proportion of
  population, 46